REAL LIFE STORIES

More Than Courage

By PATRICK LAWSON

Illustrated by

EARL SHERWAN

WHITMAN PUBLISHING COMPANY
RACINE, WISCONSIN

To all the horses and dogs that have been trying to communicate with dumb humans for thousands of years, this book is affectionately dedicated.

ACKNOWLEDGMENTS

The author wishes to extend appreciation for the assistance extended directly by Mr. Jay Barry, trainer of Gene Autry's Champ and Champ, Jr.; Mr. and Mrs. Lee Duncan, owners of Rin Tin Tin; Mr. Ralph McCutcheon, owner-trainer of Fury; Mr. Glen Randall, trainer of Roy Rogers' Trigger; and Mr. Rudd Weatherwax, owner-trainer of Lassie, all of whom generously gave of their time to contribute the information on these motion picture and television stars.

Also for the courtesy extended by the Assistant Commissioner of Scotland Yard, England; Mr. George Werntz, Jr., of The Seeing Eye, Inc.; Mr. George M. Crosier, General Manager of the Los Angeles branch of the Society for Prevention of Cruelty to Animals; and Mr. M. L. Peterson, Head Curator, Department of Armed Forces History, of the Smithsonian Institution.

CONTENTS

1

The Question

Ever since man chose the horse and dog as his helpers a few hundred centuries ago, he has been fretting over a baffling conundrum. Do these animal companions of ours think for themselves or are they dumb brutes, who follow only their instincts and our orders?

Today, those who argue these questions are divided into two camps. On one side are experts who claim that horses and dogs have little or no reasoning intelligence. In laboratory tests the mental capacity of a horse was found to be on a par with the gopher. The raccoon proved smarter than the dog.

In the opposite camp are experts of equal standing who state that horses not only have intelligence but phenomenal memories and vivid imaginations. Dogs, they say, reason with practically human ability and have even been known to talk.

Horses and dogs, undisturbed by such human notions, have gone right on serving man devotedly. Upon occasions they have acted so brilliantly that grateful emperors, armies, and nations have accorded them marble mausoleums, golden statues, and once the Silver Star and the Purple Heart.

It is around these brilliant ones, these heroes and champions of the animal world, that the controversy rages most fiercely. Can such spectacular, sustained performances, such acts of courage and heroism come out of brute instinct plus training, or do they require intelligent reasoning?

Take the case of Midnight.

Midnight held the world's bucking championship for fourteen years. Those who were present that July day at Canada's famous Calgary Stampede still talk of the stallion's first appearance. A horse, as black as midnight when the clouds have wiped out the stars, blasted out of the chute. It took only three spine-jarring, neck-snapping jumps before his rider was sprawled in the dust, dazed and helpless.

The crowd's roar of admiration suddenly changed to a gasp of horror. The horse had whirled to face his fallen rider. He looked to them now like a maddened killer. Pick-up men, whose job was to rush in and rope the frenzied animal before it could trample the rider under its slashing hoofs, stood as though they had put down roots. This had happened too quickly. They waited with the crowd in helpless silence for the man's certain death.

Then an astounding thing happened. The horse paused beside the man's prone body, sniffed it, and carefully, delicately stepped over it to trot unconcernedly toward the arena exit.

What had quieted that raging fury? That was what confused the audience. The most confused of all were the experts on animal behavior. Midnight had gone against the "original flight escape tendency," the "tendency to go berserk." These are considered basic instincts in the horse, instincts that explain why a horse which has started running is difficult to stop; why a rodeo bucker usually goes on bucking until he is quieted by the swishing ropes of the pick-up men; why many a person has been killed, not by an outlaw horse but by a perfectly normal one that went right on stampeding until the urge to violence was out of his system.

Had Midnight been acting instinctively, he would have done one of several things: slashed the rider to ribbons, kept on bucking blindly until the ropes brought him down, skittered around snorting and shying, or raced madly off in panicked flight.

In view of this, Midnight's gentle nosing of his fallen foe, his careful stepping over him, is as startling as would be the actions of a man who in one instant is trying to kill you and in the next is greeting you as an old friend.

Midnight's whole life is as bewildering to the experts as is this single action.

To begin with, considering his bloodlines, there was no reason for his being a bucker at all. This demonic art was perfected by the wild mustang, descended from the little Spanish horses brought to America by the Conquistadores when they came seeking fabled Cibola, the seven Cities of Gold. Indians say that the mustang learned its savage tricks from trying to rid itself of mountain lions that landed on its back before the big cat could sever its spine.

Midnight had thoroughbred blood in him. Thoroughbreds are high spirited but they do not make good buckers. There was Percheron blood in him too, and one can hardly imagine a Percheron turning itself into an equine cyclone. Percherons are of the breed of horses that carried the heavily armored knights on their Crusades. They are heavy-duty work horses. They run well for their weight and size, but they are slow in getting started. Midnight had split-second timing. The instant the chute gate was lifted, the black came out as though shot from a gun, rearing, kicking, sunfishing, swapping ends with such lightning speed he seemed to be doing everything at once.

What caused him to become the incarnation of lethal rage? The experts examined his colthood for the answer.

It was a spring day in 1920, in the Porcupine

Hills country near Alberta, Canada, when Midnight was brought in from winter grazing with a bunch of other horses. He was then four years old. He stood a little over fifteen hands high and weighed about thirteen hundred pounds. The thoroughbred in him showed in the proud, beautiful head, in the long, slender legs; the Percheron, in the great strength of his shoulders and his body.

Before the yipping cowhands, the black and

his companions, manes streaming, eyes frightened and flashing, raced down the new-green slope of the hill into the waiting corral. Here they milled neighing, snorting, their thudding hoofs changing the dust into yellow-white clouds.

Tall young Jim McNab, owner of the Cottonwood Ranch, watched the churning herd. He saw Midnight and marked him for his own. The summer before, the young black had been broken to the saddle and had given little trouble. It should be twice as easy to gentle him the second time. Long rests between training periods actually aid an animal to consolidate and assimilate what he has learned. McNab knew this. He knew also that after those same long months of freedom, Midnight would start bucking when a rider first climbed on his back. All range horses do if they have any spirit in them, and the black looked as though he had plenty of spirit.

Jim McNab was prepared for a fight, but he was not prepared for a combination earthquake and tornado. The third time he picked himself up out of the dirt, he confessed to the gaping cowhands, "That Midnight is just plain murder!"

Something must have happened out on that winter range to change the horse, yet he bore no claw marks of battle, no bullet crease or whip stripe. McNab could not understand it, but the young horse was beautiful and proud and he wanted him under his saddle. He set out to woo him with patience, with kindness, with gentle caresses. After a few weeks, Midnight was following him around like an overgrown dog. Eventually, he permitted McNab to saddle and ride him.

Then McNab made the mistake of letting another man mount the horse—Twenty-One Johnson. Johnson managed a precarious living traveling from ranch to ranch picking up bets that cowhands placed on their best buckers. Johnson claimed he could stay on a bolt of lightning if you could slap a saddle on it.

Midnight waited quietly until Johnson had his

feet in the stirrups. Then he went straight up, squealing, the hump in his back as big as a camel's. When he came down, his rear hoofs were kicking a hole in the sky. Johnson hauled on the reins. Midnight shot up again, jackknifing. Johnson flew off into space and kept right on going until the ground came up to meet him.

After that, Midnight refused to let even McNab ride him. It was as though the horse felt that McNab had betrayed their friendship in turning him over to a stranger. Finally Midnight was sold to Verne Elliot, who supplied equipment, men, and animals to rodeo shows.

Midnight became Elliot's star performer. He toured England, Canada, and the United States. Some said he was as great as the famous champion bucker, Steamboat, some said he was even greater.

Midnight's one aim in life was to rid himself of his rider as quickly as possible. Usually he accomplished this in three seconds. Pete Knight, himself a rodeo star, once stayed on for seven seconds.

To the audience, the horse was a wild, frenzied killer. Yet Verne Elliot claimed that in spite of the black storm Midnight seemed to the spectators, the horse knew exactly what he was doing every instant he was in front of the crowd.

During the long years of his championship, it was characteristic of Midnight that the instant he tossed his rider, he stopped bucking and trotted off, occasionally glancing mildly back at the man he had so savagely thrown. He would eat out of Mrs. Elliot's hand and was as manageable as a plow horse when she took him out for his daily exercise.

That is the story of Midnight. Nothing he did fitted into the experts' orderly slots. He became a champion bucker when his bloodlines gave him no right to buck at all. There was no cause for his actions in the kind treatment that accompanied his early training. Moreover, he did not turn outlaw. It was as though he had decided that he would freely give his friendship—as he started to do with Jim McNab—but that no man was going to master him.

What caused him to act as he did? Was it instinct or intelligent reasoning?

On the laboratory's scale of intelligence, the dog is rated higher than the horse. This is explained by the fact that the dog has been closely associated with humans for thousands of years. Nevertheless, one expert states that he has not discovered a single animal psychologist who has a very high opinion of canine intelligence. He declares that the actions of a dog trying to get into or out of a puzzle box would "make a chimpanzee snicker."

All the experts agree, however, that there are three compelling drives that motivate every living form: instinct (needs), habits (training, education), and intelligent reasoning.

Which of these impelling forces started the

dog Kola on his now famous, heroic rescue?

Mr. and Mrs. William Thress who owned Kola did not know what kind of a dog he was except that he had Husky in him.

The day Kola ceased being just a dog and became both a hero and a psychological puzzle started ominously. Great, swollen clouds blacked out the bright California sunshine. A few miles below the busy port of San Pedro, a high, flat headland thrust out into the Pacific. There the sea fretted loudly against the rocks. Lying between it and a range of low hills, the picturesque little town of Dana Point girded itself for a storm. Toward evening the storm broke. It did not rain in the usual way. It was as though the heavens had burst open. The land became a place of water.

Under drumming roofs, the people of Dana Point peered anxiously from their windows toward the hills where scrub and brush grew tall enough to hide a small deer. Lights flickered there. Through the curtain of rain they looked like fireflies. A posse of men were searching for a little lost boy.

Ronnie Sowell was five, going on six. That afternoon, he had set out to see more of the world than he could from his front yard. Through the slats in the Thress's fence, Kola watched him go. Kola knew Ronnie. Occasionally the boy came over to play with him.

When Ronnie's absence was finally noticed,

his frantic parents looked everywhere for him. Unable to find him, they notified the sheriff, and a posse was formed.

As the searching party spread out across the hills, the storm roared down upon them. Men and trees bent under it. Every ditch and gully foamed with water deep enough to drown a small boy. It became a race against time for Ronnie Sowell's life.

The men searched all night. In the gray, drenched dawn they found him. He was lying on the ground. Kola was lying on top of him. The boy was practically dry; Kola was wringing wet.

Why had Kola saved the boy? The parents asked it. The town asked it. Finally, the experts on animal behavior asked it.

The dog had been in his own yard when Ronnie left home. He was still there after Ronnie's absence was discovered. This much is known. It was some time after that he had slipped away to follow the boy.

The burrs in his shaggy coat were evidence that he had tracked Ronnie through the brush. He must have reached the boy just as the storm lashed down and known it was impossible for the child to make his way back home even with his help. So Kola had pulled himself up over Ronnie like a shaggy rug, offering his body as a shield between the little boy and the fury of the storm.

Instinct plus an incomparable nose certainly led Kola to the lost child, there is no doubt here. But no instinct could have warned the dog that Ronnie was in danger.

Kola was not responding to any previous training when he went in search of the boy. Kola had never been taught to track. He had never been taught to do much of anything except be a well-loved pet. No one had given him one of the boy's garments to sniff and said, "Go find him, Kola! Go find Ronnie!" No one had said anything to him. He was just a dog.

Kola was aware that the storm was coming. Probably he knew its exact intensity. All animals are superb weather prophets. But to connect the storm with danger to the missing child is an act of intelligence, of reasoning.

When, on April 25, 1959, the Los Angeles Branch of the Society for Prevention of Cruelty to Animals presented Kola with an award in recognition of his heroism, they also presented the experts with another puzzling problem.

What motivated Kola, instinct—or intelligence?

2

The Making of a Hero

It was July 10, 1943.

Chips, of the K-9 Corps, stood tensely beside Private John Rowell and watched the approaching Sicilian shore. Behind them, the sea was filled with the silhouettes of warships. Ahead, the blackness of pre-dawn was seared by the crimson of machine-gun tracer bullets, by the intense white-gold of flares. They stabbed and blazed in the darkness, making an erratic, beautiful, and terrible design across the fading curtain of night.

Chips saw only variations of light, for a dog is color blind.

Private Rowell, Chips's handler, heard the staccato chatter of the machine guns, the answering bark of rifles, the explosive bursts of the hand grenades. Chips heard all that and more. The normal human ear receives sound waves at a frequency between 20 and 20,000 a second. The dog hears up to 30,000. Chips flinched and whined, not in fear for he was already a veteran of the French Morocco invasion of World War II, but because he was in pain. His immediate world was filled with high-pitched, shrieking demons. He heard not only the barks and bursts of guns and grenades but their shrill, insane screams that went up and up the scale until they were lost even to the dog's sensitive ears.

Chips looked up questioningly at his handler. Private John Rowell was from Arkansas, Chips from Pleasantville, New York. Both had left families behind them when they answered the call of duty. Chips's family were the Wrens—Mr. and Mrs. Wren and their children. The girls were in grade school, but Johnny was only a baby when Chips went off to war.

Like most Americans, Chips was of mixed ancestry. His father was a Husky, his mother a cross of collie and German shepherd. Chips had inherited the best traits of all three breeds.

He felt the landing boat shudder against the shore before Rowell did. He felt it through his paws, his whole body. He hit the beach ahead of his handler.

They were just east of Licata, a place on the southern coast of Sicily. The British Eighth Army was on their right flank, Canadian troops in the center. The American Seventh Army formed the left flank. It was under the command of George S. Patton, Jr., then a lieutenant general. Chips's regiment was the Third Infantry Division.

As Chips and the other soldiers started to creep cautiously up the beach, night began to pale before the coming of dawn. Chips's nostrils flared as he winnowed the breeze. He could smell trouble ahead, but where? He could not pinpoint it. There were too many scents—the sea, the sand, the olive trees that grew on the hills; the odor of spent powder, gun oil, the men around him, their fear and tension, the smell of pain, of blood, of death.

Before them was a peasant's hut. Chips saw it only a few yards away. It appeared to be empty. Chips was trying to get a scent fix on it when the silence of the hut was shredded by a blast of machine-gun fire. Men reeled back under the impact of the bullets. Some fell and lay still beneath the slowly brightening sky.

At the time of the landing, Private John Rowell had a rifle, bayonet, helmet, and hand grenades. Chips had four fast legs and one set of sharp teeth. This is what each did with the equipment with which he had been provided.

Before that rain of leaden death, Private Rowell hit the ground along with the other men.

Chips raced straight for the machine-gun nest. He tore into the hut. There was a burst of sporadic firing. Then the gun was silent. An Italian soldier reeled out of the hut, Chips at his throat. Three other soldiers appeared after him, their hands in the air.

Rowell called Chips off before he could kill the first gunner. The dog had suffered powder burns and a crease across his head where a bullet had grazed him. In the fight inside the hut, one of the men had shot at Chips with a revolver.

The wound was not serious enough to send a soldier to the rear. Chips received first aid and remained in the front line of battle. It was fortunate that he did. That night, Chips warned Rowell that the enemy was approaching. Ten Italians were creeping along a path that led down to the beach. Private Rowell made the capture, but it was Chips who revealed their presence. This act, however, may be considered an anticlimax. Chips was already a hero.

On November 19, 1943, Chips received the Silver Star for "single-handedly eliminating a dangerous machine-gun nest and causing the surrender of its crew . . . ." The words are Captain Edward G. Paar's, who recommended the citation.

War Department regulations forbid the presentation of a medal to an animal, but regulations can be waived. Major General Lucian K. Truscott, Jr., Commander of the Third Division, waived them. "Somewhere in Italy," where Chips had been transferred, against a background of thundering guns hammering enemy emplacements, Chips was decorated while soldiers stood at rigid attention.

He was the first dog hero of the Second World War, and he created a storm of comment.

Newsmen in Italy declared that Chips had also

been awarded the Distinguished Service Cross and the Purple Heart.

William Thomas, then the national commander of the Military Order of the Purple Heart, wrote indignant letters to the President, the Secretary of War, and the Adjutant General of the United States Army. The Purple Heart, he claimed, was instituted by General George Washington for humans, not dogs.

The subject was hotly debated in Congress. It went on for three months. Some said an act of heroism was an act of heroism no matter who performed it. Others held out for a special model to be devised that could be awarded to animals, following the example of the British. In the end, it was decided that no more decorations were to be given to other than humans, though, in the case of animal acts of bravery, "appropriate citation may be published in unit general orders."

Two years later, Chips was shipped home suffering from battle fatigue. He could have boasted eight battle stars and an assault-landing arrow-head on his war ribbons—if he had worn war ribbons. Apart from the French Moroccan and Sicilian campaigns, he had served in Italy, France, Germany, and Central Europe. He had stood a twelve-hour guard watch over President Roosevelt and Winston Churchill while they shaped history during their secret meeting at Casa Blanca.

In Italy, Chips had bitten General Dwight D. Eisenhower. It happened when the General stooped to pet the hero of the Sicilian invasion. It was not Chips's fault. Eisenhower had unexpectedly touched a dog triggered by training to attack a stranger. Besides, how was Chips to know the man was a general?

However these incidents in Chips's colorful career are not debatable. They can be explained as instinct plus training. But what of those few minutes on the Sicilian Beach when Chips charged and captured the machine-gun nest? In so doing, he went against both instinct and training.

It is instinct for a dog to run from strange, loud sounds. Witness the panic of the ordinary dog racing down a street in a desperate, futile attempt to put distance between himself and the terrifying noise made by a tin can tied to his tail.

This tendency to bolt had been, of course, trained out of Chips when he entered the service —which makes his subsequent action even more remarkable. In the training of dogs for war, exactly as it is with humans, one of the first things they are taught is unswerving obedience to orders. Both men and dogs are punished if they disobey. The men are confined to the guardhouse; the dogs are made to crawl on their bellies for a few yards before their soldier companions. Both are humiliated, both lose face. As pride means as much, if not more, to a dog than to a man, it takes only a few such lessons to teach the members of the K-9 Corps not to move, even under fire, except at the command of their handlers.

Private John Rowell did not give such a command. He was too busy hitting the sand before the spray of bullets. Chips went in on his own. It was the first time since he had joined the army that he had acted without orders.

A dog will recklessly attack anyone or anything that harms his master, but Rowell was not harmed. Chips knew that. He could smell it. He also smelled the enemy in the hut, yet in French

Morocco he had caught their scent as they came creeping in out of the night to slip as silently as shadows into the officers' tents, cut their throats and steal their equipment. Chips had often given warning of their approach but he had not moved a muscle to attack until the voice or touch of his handler gave the order. Nor had he charged under the fire of the Seneghalese until he had received the word.

What made him attack the enemy in Sicily, in the face of almost certain death? Did he know the lethal damage that machine-gun nest was causing?

Was it instinct or intelligent reasoning?

The case history of Stubby is even more remarkable than that of Chips.

Stubby had his portrait painted in oils by Charles Ayres Whipple, the well-known artist.

At Mandres-en-Bassigny, he courteously offered his paw to President Woodrow Wilson when the two were introduced.

At one of the American Legion Conventions shortly after World War I, he had his picture taken with General Pershing at the General's request. Stubby did not bite General Pershing. Unlike Chips, he had not been trained for combat. Besides, he liked people, even generals.

In 1914, Germany had some three thousand dogs in the army. Russia, Belgium, France, and England also had canine battalions. The United States had none.

No one ordered Stubby to serve his country. Stubby offered himself. No one even knew where he came from, how old he was, or to whom he belonged. He simply trotted onto Yale Field where the students were training and proceeded to make friends. There was one fact about him plain enough for anyone to see: he was a bull terrier—at least most of him was.

In World War II, the army listed thirty-two breeds and crossbreeds of dogs suitable for military service. No mention is made of bull terriers.

Obviously, they were considered unfit for such arduous duties.

There was no one to explain this to the young recruits back in 1916. It would not have mattered anyway. They did not adopt the dog because of his qualifications for combat. They took him because he was Stubby. He became their mascot. Though Corporal Robert Conroy swore to one of the Military Police that the dog was a better sentry than any two men in the company, Stubby never stood guard. Conroy privately believed that should Stubby ever encounter an enemy, he would greet him with the same tail-wagging enthusiasm he showed everyone else. The MP, however, was so impressed that he helped Conroy smuggle Stubby onto the transport that was taking them to France.

Stubby was not the only dog during World War I to arrive surreptitiously in Europe. At that time, United States Army regulations forbade the transference of pets even from one training camp to another, yet a number of dogs managed to be shipped "over there." Untrained, they matched wits with the finely trained dogs of other countries in a way that made the doughboys proud.

Today, Corporal Conroy would be called Stubby's handler. Then, he was Stubby's friend. Conroy risked his Corporal's stripes to take the dog with him, and Stubby repaid him with unswerving loyalty.

Mention of World War I calls up such memories as that of General Pershing placing a wreath on Lafayette's grave saying, "Lafayette, we are here"; the fear of the whole western world when Paris was threatened by the German "Big Berthas"; the jennys and messerschmidts flown by Baron von Richtoffen and his Circus, and the almost knightly chivalry those first warriors of the air showed to the enemy.

To the average soldier, however, World War I meant trenches, tangles of barbed wire, No Man's Land, charges "over the top," and rain, seemingly unceasing rain, turning the land into slippery, oily mud, warm and sticky in summer, bone-chilling in winter. The soldiers fought, ate, and slept in mud to the accompaniment of booming artillery, the shriek of shells coming over. Their nights were lighted not by moon and stars but by the strange, white blossoms of rockets.

It was into such a scene that Stubby trotted at the heels of his master when Conroy's unit was sent to the front. Conroy was a Marine. So was Stubby.

Today, war dogs are trained to become accustomed to gunfire. Small caliber weapons are first shot off at a distance, then brought slowly nearer. Gradually heavier calibers are used until the dogs become accustomed to all types of explosives. In spite of these careful preparations, some dogs experience severe shell shock at their first encounter with enemy fire.

No one had prepared Stubby for war. He simply walked into it and accepted it as an exciting game. It was fun to duck the big shells and see which could dive into a foxhole first, man or dog. Usually Stubby won. That was because his extraordinarily sensitive ears could hear the shells long before humans could. After a while the men in his Company began watching Stubby. When he took cover, so did they. They knew when a big one was coming close, for Stubby paid no attention to the ones that went screaming overhead. There is a difference between the sound of a shell in passage and one that has begun its downward arc. Stubby was quite aware of that difference and his judgment was never wrong. Many a soldier crouched behind a barricade watching the metal splinters of an exploding shell cut the air, blessed Stubby for his warning. The odd part was that it was never a frightened warning. Stubby's dive into a foxhole was always made with the same eager excitement he would have shown going after a big, juicy bone.

It was only the wounded that troubled him. He

would rush from one to another of the moaning
men, whining in sympathy, licking at their hands
and faces. It was obvious that he wanted to help
them, but what could a dog do? Stubby found
a way.

Ambulance dogs are carefully trained to seek
out the wounded, some of whom may be half
buried in dirt, some hidden under bushes or lying
in an abandoned trench. Often rescue parties pass
them by without seeing them, especially if the

man is unconscious or too weak to make a sound. Here dogs are of inestimable value. They are sent out with a first aid kit strapped on them. Their insignia is a large red cross. When a man is badly wounded, the dogs are taught to return to the stretcher party and lead them back to the spot where the man is lying.

Stubby's method was not as suave and efficient as this, but it was just as effective. Should the enemy start laying down a death-raining barrage, Stubby would stand guard over the wounded until the firing slackened, then he would rush away in search of Conroy. When he could not find him, he would dash over to the nearest group of soldiers. By barking, racing back and forth, and hauling at their pants leg or jacket, he reported that there were men in need of help, nor could he be quieted until someone followed him back to the wounded. It is not known how many lives he saved in this way.

No one taught him to perform in this way.

Stubby worked it out for himself.

He also decided that the smell of gas was dangerous. He caught its scent a few minutes before it reached the trench where an exhausted Conroy and his fellow Marines were asleep. Stubby woke them by tearing up and down barking. The men had just enough time to slip on their masks before the silent, unseen attack was upon them.

Stubby had no mask. Conroy rushed him to the nearest hospital behind the lines. There the dog received the same aid as would have been given any soldier. It took him only a few days to recover.

By this time the whole division knew him, or knew about him. They tried to get a mask for Stubby, but none had been made that would fit a bull terrier's face. Stubby did not really need one. Gas attacks were few, and he did not smell that strange, alarming scent again.

An important part of the training of combat dogs is familiarizing them with the sight, sound, and smell of the enemy before they meet him in battle. Stubby had to learn that scent for himself and distinguish it from the thousand other odors about him. The fact that an Oriental or a Moroccan or an African may smell different than a Caucasian is understandable, but in what way does a German differ from a Frenchman, an Englishman, or an American?

Stubby knew. One night he tore out of the dugout and captured a spy by sinking his teeth into the seat of the man's pants. It is highly improbable that the dog was alerted by the spy's scent of fear, which is a real, tangible odor. Stubby lived in the midst of a constant aroma of fear. Though men may talk, act, and even think bravely, fear is there when the big shells start exploding in a geyser of mud, metal scraps—and human bodies. Whatever the odor was that reached Stubby's highly discriminating nose, it said, "Enemy!"

By this time, Stubby was the hero of the A.E.F. He had his own service jacket. It was a chamois coat embroidered with all the Allied flags. The women of Chateau-Thierry made it for him.

When the war ended, Stubby went back home with his master.

The retraining of a war dog for civilian life is as long and arduous as his training for combat. Where before he was taught to be suspicious of strangers, he must now regard them in a friendly manner or, at least, indifferently. Never again must he give that deadly, silent leap for a person's throat. In the event that the dog cannot make the adjustment he is shot, for he is too dangerous to be turned loose. If he does respond to the retraining satisfactorily, he is demobilized and his military papers and records are sent home with him.

Stubby was not demobilized. He was not officially a Marine. He did not have to be taught not to attack strangers. No one was a stranger to him. Now that the war was over, they were all friends. So Stubby simply trotted up the ship's gangplank like a seasoned traveler. Unlike Chips, who was always seasick, Stubby took his daily constitutional on deck and never missed a meal.

Back on home soil, he was made a life member of the American Red Cross and the American Legion, the Eddy Glover Post, No. 6, New Britain, Connecticut. He attended the American Legion meetings and led their parades wearing his embroidered service jacket. When his master stayed at New York's Hotel Majestic—where dogs were never allowed—Copeland Townsend, the owner, gravely shook "hands" with Stubby and had him put his paw print on the register. The choicest cuts of meat were sent to his room, and everything was "with the compliments of Mr. Townsend."

However, Stubby's most extraordinary act of bravery was performed several years after he and Conroy had returned to civilian life. It happened in Paris, where Conroy was making a nostalgic visit. Stubby, of course, went, too.

Man and dog strolled down the boulevard, the

man remembering the many leaves he had spent in this gay capital sitting lazily in the sun at one of the sidewalk café tables, browsing through the bookstalls on the Left Bank, going boating on the Seine with Mlle. Fifi, or was it Kiki, or Marie? The dog was sniffing the fascinating odors of the trunks of the chestnut trees and watching the pretty French poodles pass, ribbon bows in their hair. His eyes approved but his nose probably rebelled. French women have a habit of drenching their pets in perfume, and dogs generally dislike any odor that has alcohol in it.

Then Conroy and Stubby started across the street. Suddenly Stubby tore his leash out of Conroy's hand, streaked to the opposite curb and hurled himself upon a young girl who had just stepped into the line of traffic. Girl and dog went careening to one side as a weaving, speeding taxi tore down upon them. The car grazed them, but the damage was slight.

Conroy had not seen the danger the girl was

in. The dog had, and he acted instantly.

When Stubby died on April 4, 1926, a plaster cast was made of his body to encase his ashes, and was presented to the Smithsonian Institution, Washington, D.C., where it is on display as a tribute to his heroism.

Chips of the K-9 Corp was highly trained. In capturing the machine-gun nest, he apparently went against both instinct and training.

Stubby's unusual courage, his cheerfulness in the midst of battle, his concern over the wounded was not the result of natural instinct, nor was he responding to previous training. He was not trained when he appeared out of nowhere that day at Yale Field. None of the soldiers trained him except perhaps to "shake hands." They were too busy playing with him and vying for his affections.

Could it be said then that Stubby acted through intelligent reasoning?

3

Drumming Hoofs

Henry Wynmalen, that master of the art of schooling and riding, declares that a horse has both an excellent memory and imagination. Especially does it remember a person, place, or event that has hurt or frightened it. When it approaches that spot, that individual, or even catches the scent, remembrance returns to it so very vividly that it appears to be almost as frightened the second time as it was the first.

A story is told of Prince, a strawberry roan. In 1878, Prince and his owner, Chester Evans, were trying to outrace fifteen Cheyenne Indians to Fort Monument on Smoky Hill River in Kansas. Both were wounded by Indian arrows; both recovered. Evans remembered the incident, but he could never pass an Indian without flinching. Prince hated redskins for the rest of his life.

Twenty years after man and horse had encountered the Cheyennes, Prince was grazing in a pasture. Suddenly he flung up his head and sniffed the wind. To Evans' surprise, the horse began to snort and paw the ground, furiously challenging some unseen enemy. Later, Evans discovered that a group of Oklahoma Indians had stopped at the little town of Lebo. Lebo was half a mile from Prince's pasture.

This instinctive tendency to avoid that which has frightened or hurt them may be overcome by the horse's training, say the experts. If firm, kindly treatment has produced confidence in the rider, the horse will sense that the man will not force him into danger and will be persuaded to conquer his old fears.

In view of this, the action of cavalry horses and their courage in battle is all the more remarkable. A horse can be taught to ignore gunfire, but how can he continue to have confidence in a master who deliberately leads him into a situation where he is severely wounded?

In cavalry warfare, it was part of military technique to shoot a man's mount from under him. A horse was considered as dangerous an enemy as a man. Yet such horses returned again and again to the tumult of battle, the roar of the cannon, the deadly swish and clash of steel.

When one cavalry officer encountered a mounted enemy, consider the actions of their horses. As the men fought from the saddle, the horses did not stand still. They were constantly maneuvering that their masters might be in the best

position for the downward saber stroke or the
equally terrible sideswipe. It is impossible to
believe that in the midst of a life-and-death duel,
the rider was giving his horse instructions either
by hand or knee. This he may have done during
training, but no two duels were ever identical.
The horse had to make his own decisions. He
made them, often brilliantly, keeping a wary eye
on the enemy's horse, circling when he circled,
then swinging in so close that the men fought
knee to knee.

This action perhaps is the most remarkable of
all. Instinct in animals demands that they do not
come within striking range of an opponent unless
they are prepared to attack. There is a set line,
varying with each animal, which marks the boun-
dary of what is called "flight safety." Up to that
line, they can turn and run if they desire. Cross
that line and they place themselves in danger in
two ways: they must fight or run. If they choose
to run, they must *pass* the enemy, which leaves

their back and rear exposed to slashing hoof or raking claw.

Even in domesticated animals, this "flight safety" line controls their actions. A horse shies from a strange object. He may be afraid. Again, he may be merely retreating to that invisible line where instinct informs him he has enough distance between himself and the object to permit him to turn and run without fear of an attack from flank or rear.

Here in battle are two horses who should be maddened by the sounds and excitement of conflict. To add to the confusion, other cavalry horses are rushing by them as line after line charges, their thundering hoofs making the earth into a hollow drum. But the two horses of the dueling officers do not follow the others' flight. Neither do they pay any attention to the bullets spurting little puffs of dust at their heels.

It may be said that the flight tendency has been trained out of them, but there can have been no previous training in regard to wounds. What prevents a pain-crazed horse from bolting? Yet he will hold his position as long as he is able to stand. When the rider too is hurt, many a horse has carried the man safely to the rear before he, himself, collapsed.

Sam was one of General William Tecumseh Sherman's favorite mounts. Sherman rode him in many battles. The horse was wounded several times. In spite of this, Sam was so quiet under

fire that the General could write his orders sitting in the saddle.

General George Meade purchased a horse named Baldy. Baldy had been severely wounded in the first battle of Bull Run and had barely recovered when he came into Meade's possession. With Meade, he went through the seven days of bitter fighting that raged around Richmond in 1862. He was in the battle of Antietam and received such a deep wound in his neck that he was left for dead on the field. Later, he was discovered trying to crop a little grass and was brought in for treatment, which in those days more often killed than cured.

After Baldy recovered, he went right back into conflict to take his part in the battles of Chancellorsville, Fredericksburg, and Gettysburg. During the battle of Gettysburg, he calmly carried Meade for two days without rest, conquering both the tendency to flight and his fatigue in order to perform his duty. Then, near the climax of the fight, the horse was struck by a bullet that almost ended his life.

By the time he was well again, the war was over. He lived to follow the funeral cortege that took his master to his grave, the General's empty saddle on his back, the General's boots reversed in the stirrups.

No mention of famous cavalry horses would be complete without Alexander the Great's favorite and friend, Bucephalus. Alexander thought so much of the horse that he named a town after him. Bucephalus, meaning "oxhead," was ink black with a white star on his forehead. It was said that he had one gray eye and one brown.

For sixteen years he carried his master into that part of the battle where the fighting was fiercest. He had to face more than the humming flight of arrows, the clang of sword on shield, the charge of other horses. In India, he met the terrible war elephants.

Long, sharp knives, curved like great scythes,

bristled from the leather skirts that hung almost to the heels of these elephants. When they rushed through the enemies' lines, they were like huge mowing machines. Expert archers filled the howdahs on their backs sending down twanging death on the enemy below. The trumpetings of the elephants shook the air even as their ponderous feet shook the earth. Their pipe-organ bellows changed to ear-splitting screams when they became enraged. Their trunks shot out like writhing serpents to pluck a man off a horse, lift him high in the air, and smash him on the ground.

Bucephalus was not prepared to meet such monsters. They must have terrified him, but he never turned and ran, except once. That was also in India.

Alexander, with his usual youthful impatience, was several yards ahead of his army, facing the massed forces of an Indian prince. There had been one attack already. The battle lines had drawn back to re-form. Now Alexander again ordered his soldiers to advance. The hot rays of the sun struck sparks from his bronze helmet, his shield and breastplate, from the short-bladed, bronze sword in his hand. His knees, under the white, pleated kirtle, gripped the sides of the sweating, black horse. There may have been a small blanket between them, there may have been nothing, for ancient pictures on urns and vases show both Greeks and Macedonians riding bareback.

Alexander urged the horse forward. For the first time in sixteen long, turbulent years, Bucephalus refused to obey. Angrily, Alexander repeated the order. The horse whirled suddenly, and at a gallop, bore his astounded master back through his own scattering lines. Halting, the horse kneeled as he had been trained to do that Alexander might dismount. Then Bucephalus rolled over dead. For the first time, Alexander discovered, to his almost inconsolable grief, that the valiant horse had been fatally wounded in the first encounter with the enemy.

Bucephalus disobeyed Alexander's orders that he might carry his master to a place of safety before he died. Was this instinct? Certainly it was not the result of training. Alexander never showed his back to the enemy, and never before had Bucephalus taken his master to the rear.

This in itself is remarkable, but how is one to explain the action of Two Bits?

Two Bits was never in any historic battle, nor did a famous general ever ride him. The highest he ever rose in the ranks was to the saddle of a captain—Captain Charles A. Curtis. Until then, the big bay had known a dozen masters for he was one of a cavalry pool at Fort Craig, New Mexico.

It was between the 1870's and '80's. The United States was trying to persuade the Indians to stay on the reservations appointed to them. The Indians, largely Apaches, Comanches, and Navahos, were not taking kindly to the Government's methods of armed persuasion. Bands of warriors still roamed the high mesas. In the vast emptiness of the landscape, a troop of soldiers could be seen for miles, but the Indians seemed to melt into the background. The old-timers had a saying, "When you don't see an Indian, you're looking right at him."

That was the reason for the forts with their high stockades. They were constantly being raided by the Indians, more for the horses than the men. Among the redskins, it was considered an act of greater courage to slip a horse out of a corral than a knife into a soldier.

It was at Fort Craig that Two Bits caught his first scent of the red enemy. Here, too, he was given his name.

Men cannot be continually on nerve-taut guard without some relaxation, and so a race was arranged one bright June day when the great half dome of the sky was filled with clouds as small and white as baby lambs.

The swiftest horses of the Mounted Rifles had already been chosen by the riders. One horse was left, a big bay. An Irish fifer boy named Cain decided to ride him. As they trotted to the starting line, a soldier shouted derisively, "I wouldn't give two bits for that horse."

Two Bits won by three lengths.

Six years later Cain, now a sergeant, was to meet Two Bits under vastly different conditions.

The horse had been included in a bunch that were considered no longer fit for cavalry service. Soldiers transferred from New Mexico to Arizona had brought the herd with them to be sold. It was a seven-hundred mile trek. At the end, the horses looked even more decrepit than they had at the start of the march. At auction, they brought about five dollars a head. Two Bits came into the possession of a new and brutal master. Cain, then serving at Fort Whipple, in Arizona, came upon the horse lying on the ground starved to the point of emaciation. A man was standing over

him beating him unmercifully.

Sergeant Cain sprang to the horse's defense before he recognized Two Bits. The owner was willing to give him up to avoid a fight, and Sergeant Cain took him back to the fort. With him, he took a horse-sized problem.

Fort Whipple stood on the slope of one of the wooded hills surrounding the town of Prescott. Spread out below were corrals for the horses and mules. There were also three hundred head of cattle and a thousand sheep offering constant temptation to marauding Indians. It would have seemed that with all these animals there would have been room for one more, that Two Bits could have been easily lost among them, but every one was marked and every horse known.

Cain was fully aware that the Army would not accept the broken-down old horse into the cavalry pool, and he could not afford to keep him himself, not on a sergeant's pay. It was not a matter of selling him that bothered Cain, it was finding him a kind, understanding master.

Cain's captain was the ideal owner for Two Bits, but would Captain Curtis buy him? Cain needed money for a special reason; he had to have it. "I'll let you have him for five dollars, sir," he told Curtis, "and you'll be gettin' the finest horse on the post." Curtis laughingly refused, but Cain's Irish tongue proved so eloquent that the captain finally agreed.

During the next few weeks, the deal he had

made with his sergeant slipped from Curtis' mind. He was surprised when Cain appeared with a beautiful bay, groomed from mane to fetlock, sleek and filled out—on the oats the captain's five dollars had purchased for him. Two Bits and Curtis fell in love with each other at first sight.

The horse renewed his acquaintance with the red men on the marches the captain and his troop made in pursuit of Indians who had swooped down on village and wagon train to loot and kill. He knew the wolf bark of the Apache, the high-pitched yip of the charging Comanche that raised the hair right up with its insane clamor. He knew, too, the peaceful times when Curtis would take him for a canter among the pine trees that broke up the hard, bright Arizona sunshine into soft, cathedral shafts of light. He caught the scent of deer and bear long before he saw them in swift or lumbering flight.

Perhaps the happiest days were those when Curtis went fishing. Then the man would flick the quiet, shadowed pools for trout, and the horse would graze nearby. On one such day the succulent grass tempted Two Bits farther away than usual from his master. He was cropping contentedly when the wind suddenly said, "Danger!" Instantly, Two Bits wheeled and raced back to Curtis. The captain did not stop to question. He flung himself into the saddle and they were off. A yelp of frustrated fury broke out behind them. A war party of mounted Apaches burst from cover and raced in pursuit.

Two Bits outran them. As the fort came into view, the disgruntled Indians slackened their speed and turned back.

A second time, Curtis was attacked by Indians lying in ambush. The shot, creasing the captain's coat collar, took both horse and rider by surprise. Two Bits involuntarily shied. Curtis was thrown. Before the captain had hit the ground, the horse froze, waiting for him to remount. The smell of the Indians was strong in Two Bits' nostrils, along with the smell of rifle powder. He could have reverted to instinctive flight, but he made no move until his master was in the saddle. Even then he did not run. He walked slowly, carefully away from the ambush while Curtis, pistol in hand, waited for the Indians to show themselves. It was as though the horse was giving the captain the opportunity to return the fire, as though he knew how many there were, that they were not the overpowering force in the first attack. It was not until rifle space was between them and the enemy that Two Bits broke into a run. Behind them three Apaches rose from the bushes, the black dots and blue crescents on their faces showing them to be painted for war.

However, Two Bits did not prove the heights of his courage and heroism when Curtis was riding him. At that time, he carried a comparative stranger on a dangerous mission.

Express riders were being found scalped, the contents of their postal pouches scattered over the blood-stained ground. This happened so often that riders could no longer be hired for that stretch of service between Arizona and New Mexico. Cavalrymen had to deliver the mail. They went out first in pairs, later in groups. Even then they were cut down.

The situation was becoming increasingly tense. Captain Curtis knew it all too well. A dispatch had been received that morning from San Francisco. The nature of its contents required that it be sent on at once to Santa Fe. By whom? Who would venture into the heart of Apache country?

The captain advertised for a civilian rider, offering the highest pay. There were no takers. Curtis felt that he could spare no more men from his troop. There were too few now to risk sending out four or five to possible slaughter.

Then Sergeant Porter of the Quartermaster's Department volunteered to carry the dispatch on one condition—that he should be allowed to ride Two Bits.

The horse had made quite a name for himself at the fort. Not only had he twice saved the captain's life, but he had won a race which even his owner thought he had no chance of winning. It was Sergeant Cain who insisted that Two Bits be entered.

"Why that horse must be twenty years old!" Curtis had protested.

"Sure, and the older he grows, the faster he goes," Cain answered.

And Cain was on his back, as he had been in the first race at Fort Craig, when Two Bits romped home with daylight showing between him and the rest of the field.

Now Sergeant Porter wanted to ride Two Bits. He said he would feel safe with him. Curtis was loathe to give him the horse. He felt that he was sending Two Bits to almost certain death. Yet there was the dispatch that had to be delivered. Reluctantly he agreed.

For three bitter cold nights, Sergeant Porter

slept in his blankets under the blazing stars while Two Bits stood watch, now grazing, now half dozing, but with ears and nose constantly alert.

On the fourth day, they reached a broad military road that crossed over a low hill and dropped down to a wide, flat plain. However, a flash flood had wiped out a part of the road and tumbled rocks down on it from the hill. Wagons and mule trains had made a new path around this point. It skirted the hill instead of going over it, and a mile beyond rejoined the original military road.

Ordinarily, Porter would have taken the smoother, easier way, but now he hesitated. He could not see what lay on the other side of the hill. Unable to make up his mind, he left the decision to the horse. Two Bits promptly chose the original, boulder-strewn road. He made his way up the slope with unusual caution. Near the crest, he halted, rigid, ears pricked forward. Porter, dismounting, crept to the top of the hill. On the other side were four Indian ponies, partially

concealed in the brush. Porter did not see the Indians, he did not expect to but he knew they were there. They were waiting for the Express Rider—for him.

If Two Bits had not chosen the hill path, if he had not alerted Porter to the danger lying ahead, the sergeant would have unknowingly ridden straight into ambush.

Porter led the horse back down the hill to the road made by the wagon wheels. He could not detour around the Indians. It would take too much time, another day maybe. But he figured that if he surprised the war party, he could pass them before they had recovered enough to hoot. He moved silently forward on foot, the horse right behind him. Then, when he was in sight of the ambush, he flung himself into the saddle. Two Bits broke into a ground-eating gallop.

An Indian pony raised its head, snorting. Porter shot it. The other three Indians jumped for their horses. Yelping, they tore after their quarry.

Two Bits' stride lengthened, but he was carrying too much weight—the man, a twenty-pound mail sack, three blankets, an overcoat, a carbine, and rations for another three days.

Bullets started whining around him. One struck him in the flank. He kept on. Porter was hit in the shoulder. He fired back. One of the three Indians made a half arc over the rump of his galloping horse. The two remaining Indians fired. A bullet smashed Porter's right hand. He switched his gun to his left and fired back. The carbine of the second Indian, stolen from a dead soldier, flew up in the air.

Now there was only one Indian left. He came on firing, gaining on the laboring Two Bits and his rider.

In a final act of desperation, Porter wheeled Two Bits and shot the third Indian's horse. Apache and pony fell together. Two Bits spun around and raced on. Blood oozed from several bullet wounds. The sergeant did not notice this.

He was too badly wounded himself. At last he pulled the horse to a halt, slid down from the saddle—and pitched forward on his face.

Two Bits nosed him. When Porter did not respond, the horse lifted its head and asked questions of the wind. It answered, "Smoke—and men —straight ahead." Two Bits broke into a gallop.

The guard of a Government train, huddled around their fire, looked up in surprise as the blood-streaked horse trotted up to them, mail pouch strapped to an empty saddle. They ran to catch hold of the bridle. Two Bits shied, snorting. Turning, he trotted back the way he had come. When the soldiers did not follow, he halted, looking over his shoulder.

The camp was immediately alerted. Mounted soldiers swung in behind the wounded horse, waiting for him to take the lead. Two Bits moved forward, staggered—and died.

The full story of his heroic ride was pieced together from the men of the Government train and Sergeant Porter. Rescued, Porter was sent to Fort Wingate where he recovered.

Granted that training might have taken Two Bits to the encamped soldiers, what made the dying horse attempt to lead a rescue party back to the man who was not even his master—instinct or intelligence?

Two Bits was given a soldier's burial under shading pines where twenty-one cavalry men already lay sleeping. Each grave was covered by stones, but the cairn above Two Bits was the largest. Soldiers passing that way never failed to dismount and add another stone to the mound in tribute to the heroic horse that wasn't worth "two bits."

4

Guardians of the Law

"To the dog," says a Chinese proverb, "the world is one vast smell."

This is true of all dogs, but not all dogs make good trackers. Trainers of police dogs say that few have the keenness of scent necessary to be a canine member of the police force. This is comparable to saying that while nearly everyone can sing, only exceptional singers can become grand opera stars. Among the dogs who have that sharpness of scent, there will be those that are too "flittery" to keep their minds on their work. Ability, declare these trainers, must be backed by interest, patience, and intelligence.

The virtuoso of scent is supposed to be the bloodhound. As a breed, this type of dog is very old. Romans used them to track down animals wounded in the chase. Some historians maintain that the name of this specie came from those ancient trails of blood they followed. Others believe that originally they were called "blooded hounds" to distinguish them from mixed breeds or mongrels.

Whatever the source, the name itself is sufficient to arouse deep, ancestral fears. The very baying of hounds creates a sense of terror. These dogs do not bark, they give tongue with deep, mournful organ notes that issue from their chests. One visions them, noses to the ground, relentlessly following an escaped criminal or runaway slave.

Above them, tree branches clash in the wind while scudding clouds across the moon give warning of the coming storm. Then, at the edge of a dark swamp, the hunted man is cornered. The hounds close in, fangs showing in savage snarls. One hound leaps, there is the click of snapping jaws and the terrible screams of the victim are stilled.

What is wrong about this picture is that bloodhounds do not attack their quarry. Naturally, any

dog will jump a person given the proper provocation, but to expect a bloodhound to capture a criminal is like expecting a concert pianist to move the piano onto the stage. Bloodhounds are specialists. They consider that they have done their duty when they have their prey cornered. The rest is up to the humans who follow them.

Almost everyone in the English-speaking world is familiar with the incident in *Uncle Tom's Cabin* where the slave, Eliza, attempts to escape across a stretch of ice, her baby in her arms. Behind her, hot on her trail, come slavering hounds. Various illustrations of the book have shown these dogs as bloodhounds. When *Uncle Tom's Cabin* was made into a play, stage managers, in casting these canine roles, made the same error. Actually, bloodhounds did not make their appearance in the United States until 1888, some thirty-six years after Harriet Beecher Stowe's book was published. Before then an ugly, mixed breed of dog, part mastiff, was used for tracking. Being brought over from Cuba, it was known as a "Cuban hound."

Another error is the belief that bloodhounds are both relentless and infallible. Men who have worked with these dogs continually warn that the handler must be as alert as the hound. If he sees a footprint or a bit of crushed foliage, he must call the dog's attention to it. Should the hound become confused because of a mingling of odors, as where a large number of people have trampled the ground, the handler should not give up. Instead, he should take the dog beyond the spot and "recast" him, that is, give him another chance to pick up the scent.

There are some critics who say that no play manager would hire bloodhounds to trail Eliza because the hounds could not find their way across the stage. This is an undeserved jibe at a breed that has for centuries proved its worth. But if bloodhounds were as good as legend and fiction have pictured them, they would head the preferred list of the police forces of the world. Instead, it is the German shepherd, with the Doberman pinscher as runner-up.

Exacting requirements eliminate many of even these two breeds. A good police dog must be strong but not rough, friendly but not so affectionate that it will greet strangers with tail-wagging enthusiasm. If it wants to play all the time, it is a sign that it is mentally immature and it will be ruled out, though a morose dog is equally rejected. In police dogs, intelligence is sought first, and next a gaiety of disposition. In fact, say the trainers, gaiety is a sure sign of intelligence.

Bloodhounds are not gay. Specially bred for a certain type of work, they have not been man's best friend or his companion. Though gentle with those they know, they are high-strung and easily upset, and the slightest noise starts them baying until they sound like Cerberus at the gates of Hades. This alone would prevent them from being chosen for police service. Here dogs, like

men, are often required to work in complete
silence. The instinctive habit of barking, so much
a part of canine nature, must be controlled.

In the United States, German shepherds are
often called "police dogs." This is as incorrect as
to call them "Alsatians," a name by which they
are known throughout Europe. The English are
responsible for that. After World War I they had
a hearty dislike of anything German, but they
liked this breed of dogs. Not being able to change
the name of a nation, they changed that of the
German shepherd.

Police dogs are those dogs specially trained to
be guardians of the law and may include any
breed from French poodle to great Dane.

Here again, fiction has distorted fact. Authors
have depicted trained police dogs to be as deadly
as a loaded gun. Only its master's hand on the
leash prevents it from turning into a raving mon-
ster. In view of this, it is interesting to note that
when a canine member of England's famed Scot-

land Yard goes off duty, he accompanies his master home. There he is accepted as part of the family, and while Junior is not permitted to take the dog to bed with him, Junior can play with him without losing a hand.

A savage, vicious dog would not be tolerated on the police force any more than a vicious man. These dogs are not trained for the sole purpose of tracking down criminals; they also find lost children and old ladies. The real police dog is a gentleman—a gentleman with a twinkle in his eye. One does not, of course, walk up to a police dog and pat it, but then one does not pat Officer O'Hannihan either.

Police dogs are taught to perform as many as eighty different acts, from simple "heeling" and "setting" to scaling ten-foot walls and jumping through burning windows. Trainers say that the most difficult part is to get a dog, especially a German shepherd, to attack a man. Shepherds are a friendly breed though their friendliness is tempered by a natural pride and dignity. They have worked in close association with men for hundreds of years and if they do attack, it is in defense.

When, during the training of a German shepherd, a stranger leaps out of ambush and waves a sack under its nose, the dog at first simply dodges. Mutely he appeals to his handler as though saying, "Now what am I supposed to do?" It is only when he has tried every other way to escape that annoying piece of cloth that he seizes it in his teeth. Then, to his bewildered astonishment, he is extravagantly petted and praised. From then on, he is patiently taught the right way to attack. This is not the deadly jump for the throat but a direct aim at the gun arm. If the leap is well executed, the weight of the dog swings the man's arm behind his back very much like a jujitsu hold. The man's sleeve will be torn, he may even be scratched, but that is as far as it goes. The German shepherd has had such long

practice in controlling a rampaging sheep by getting a good, firm grip on its wool that it has become second nature to hold anything in its mouth without crushing. German shepherds have been known to help a mother cat carry her newborn kittens from one place to another without leaving a single tooth mark.

In spite of this, the fear of dogs, particularly dogs as big as the bloodhound and shepherd, continues to haunt mankind. There are several prisons in the United States where canine guards patrol the grounds right beside the human guards. In one, a riot was quelled simply by the warden's threat to "call out the dogs." In another penitentiary several hundred desperate criminals attempting a prison break promptly changed their minds when faced with half a dozen guard dogs. The dogs were not snarling or lunging savagely against their leashes; they were just sitting quietly beside their handlers, but at sight of them, the prisoners laid down their weapons and surrendered.

Again, in Berlin two police dogs stopped a free-for-all in a saloon. One of their handlers had been knocked unconscious, the other had gone to telephone for help. The dogs plunged alone into the melee of swinging fists, bottles and chairs. When the second policeman came back with reinforcements, every man in the saloon was backed against the wall, held motionless merely by fear for the two dogs were simply sitting in the middle of the floor. That was all they were doing, just sitting and looking.

It may be argued that this age-old fear goes back into the dawn of time when cavemen were stalked by wolves and jackals. But historians and paleontologists are convinced that our neolithic ancestors, far from dreading these animals, used to leave bits of meat out in order to make them remain close to camp that their barking might warn the men of the approach of a woolly mammoth or a saber-toothed tiger.

Probably the fear of large dogs is based upon the animal's unpredictability. A person generally knows what another person will do in a given situation. He does not know what a dog will do. As in the well-known cartoon, a man facing a dog that is both barking and wagging its tail may very well ask, "Which end am I to believe?"

That, say canine experts, depends upon the man. If he is afraid, the dog will smell this scent of fear and very likely bite him. What produces this scent in animals and humans is unknown. It has been suggested that it may be the adrenal glands. A few humans have caught a whiff of it and have described it as "acrid," "sweetish putre-fication," "the odor of death." They say it stings the nostrils, and if it does this to a human, it would hurt a dog's super-sensitive nose a thou-sand times more. It may be pain rather than viciousness that causes a dog to attack the stran-ger who gives off this odor. Certainly the smell must be unmistakable and alarming.

A Swiss police dog going along a country road with his handler passed half a dozen farmers. He had never seen any of them before but he did not favor them with so much as a glance. However, when he neared a big haystack, he stopped sud-denly and alerted his handler. The puzzled po-liceman dug into the hay and hauled out a wanted criminal. Neither dog nor officer was looking for him. He gave himself away by the scent of fear.

In British Columbia, Cliffe, a canine member

of the Royal Canadian Mounted Police, nosed out a murderer from under a stack of hay. The hay was in a barn that the human police had already searched. They had poked about in it but with all their prying, the hunted man had been buried too deep for them to find. The dog caught his fear scent in spite of all the other odors which the average barn collects through its years of use.

Even without fear, every moving thing leaves a trail which a dog can follow as easily as we can follow footprints. But of what is this trail composed? Some say it is microscopic bits of molecular matter that is shed in passing and falls to the ground. If so, then each infinitesimal scrap must be impregnated with its owner's distinctive odor, which is unlike any other odor in the world. Scientists, testing the scenting ability of a dog, had the dog's trainer lightly touch the end of a stick with one finger. Then they sent the trainer down the hall to hide in a closet while they covered the stick with a paint reeking with banana oil. On top of that, they put mustard, catsup, perfume, and oil of cloves. This stick was given to the dog. He sniffed it, and two minutes later was barking at the door of the closet in which his trainer was concealed.

Wigger, a noble-looking German shepherd, was called in to solve a baffling case in a Swiss village where the principal industry was the raising of chinchilla rabbits. These creatures are so small that many, many skins go into the making of a full-length chinchilla coat. When finished, such a coat may cost from thirty to forty thousand dollars. So it was a matter of grave concern when the villagers discovered that someone or something had been going from farm to farm breaking into the hutches and wantonly slaughtering these expensive little animals.

Now there is nothing that the average dog likes to do more than chase rabbits, and here was Wigger right in the midst of these fascinating creatures. But Wigger was a member of the police

force and knew it. He kept his mind, and nose, strictly on his work. From hutch to hutch he went, across fields, through woods until he came to a farmhouse. There he led his handlers straight to the kennel of a large chained dog. Finally, the dog's owner admitted that he had been letting the dog loose at night to guard the house. Instead of guarding, the animal had gone on a murdering spree.

Here is a case of one dog trailing another, of following the individual scent through farms and fields and woods to the culprit's kennel, and pointing him out among all the many forms of life that inhabited that area.

Smoky, another canine member of the Canadian Mounties, trailed a three-year-old girl over ground that had been trampled by more than a hundred searchers. How did he pick out her scent from all the other odors?

To humans, smells mix and mingle. Unless one odor is much stronger than the others, there is no differentiation. To an animal, odors lie in stratas, in layers. Let us translate this ability to smell into sound. We are following the *sound* of a bell that strikes the same note as the middle C on a piano. All about us are other bells chiming, some loud, some soft, but none of them giving off the same note as the bell which we are following. By a superhuman effort, we concentrate only on that one note. It rings clearly and we rush toward it; it dies to a whisper while other bells increase their clamor. We stop to listen tensely. There it is, just barely audible! Off we go again, and if we are on the right track, the sound of the bell increases in volume.

In much the same way a dog follows an odor trail. When the odor is overwhelmed by stronger smells, he must pause and sniff around, just as we would pause and listen to a diminishing sound.

Chief, a police dog, found an illicit whisky still under a garbage dump. In spite of the violent odors arising from the refuse, the scent of whisky was caught by the dog's delicate nostrils. Egon, a police dog in Nova Scotia, not only located a still, he led his handler to a farmhouse and into a room full of people. There he unerringly pointed out the moonshiner by sitting down in front of him and gazing at him accusingly.

If this scent trail is comprised of minuscule fragments of matter that fall to the ground, how can a dog pick up the trail from the air? Yet, when a trail is fresh, even bloodhounds go along with their heads up ignoring whatever may have been deposited upon the earth. Do these scented fragments first hang for a while in the air and then settle? If so, what becomes of them if they fall upon water?

Still water, state dog trainers, holds the scent as strongly as soil, rapid water washes it away. A dog crossing a swiftly running stream must be recast so that he can pick up the trail again. But what happens when it rains and the ground is running with water?

In New Brunswick, Cliffe, the same dog that located the murderer under a pile of hay in the barn, found a local doctor who was unconscious by trailing him through thick brush in a driving rainstorm.

It is conceivable that this effluvium which living things cast off might settle in the cracks and crevasses of the earth, but pavement is another matter. Crossed and recrossed by thousands of feet, would these fragments not adhere to shoes and be carried away? If they are, they must leave behind some trace. Scotland Yard dogs have trailed their quarry through the heart of London, while Egon of the Mounties led his handler to a child that had been lost in the middle of the bustling city of Halifax.

Cold slows the molecular action of matter. With that slowing, odor is subdued until, at the point of freezing, odor ceases to exist, at least as far as the human nose is concerned. Yet one dog dug down through ten inches of snow and came

up with a button, a single coat button. Later the
button was introduced as evidence in court and
sent a man to jail. Smelling a button under ten
inches of snow places a dog's scenting ability in
the realm of the miraculous.

However, in the eyes of experts, Dale of Cawsalta performed an even more remarkable feat.
At first Dale was just a dog belonging to Sergeant
John Cawsey of the Royal Canadian Mounted
Police. Cawsey had trained the German shepherd
to help him in his work. In that vast area com-
prising northwestern Canada, where a few officers of the law must patrol hundreds of square
miles of territory, any aid that can be given is
gratefully received. Then within twenty-four
hours Dale won international fame by tracking
a wanted man hidden in shoulder-high wheat, and
found a lost child after more than a hundred men
had given up the search. Both acts were accomplished in pouring rain. Dale became a member
of the Legion of Honor of the Dog World of the

United States and received a citation from the Humane Society. What was even more important to the dog and his master, the Canadian police officials decided to accept dogs into the force. Dale became the first canine member of the Mounties, and thereafter was officially known as K470.

Dale loved children. When he found the lost child sodden with rain and exhaustion, he anxiously licked the tiny girl's face. He became known

as the "Silent Partner," and children in trouble sought him out. A small girl who had lost some money her mother had given her to pay a bill went to Dale for help instead of to Sergeant Cawsey. Dale caught the scent from the air, bounded away, and returned a few minutes later with the money. Apparently his joy was as great as the child's for he allowed her to hug him until she practically choked him.

During Dale's long and honorable career, he was instrumental in bringing to justice the murderers of two Mounties, and he led his master to safety through a blizzard. However, it was in the Canmore, Alberta, arson case that he brilliantly performed under circumstances any animal expert would have said were impossible. Some person or persons unknown had sprayed gasoline on the cellar walls of a farmer's house and set fire to it. The only evidence was a piece of underwear and a swab of cotton. Both reeked with gasoline fumes, yet after sniffing them for a minute, Dale confidently started off on the trail of the arsonist. What was even more astounding, he tracked the man in a howling *dust storm*.

Dust seems to disturb a dog as much as it does a human. Bloodhounds, following a scent, will stop at any running water and wash their noses, just as an opera star sprays his throat before going on stage. Bloodhounds would have been lost in that swirling Alberta storm, but neither gasoline fumes nor dust could stop Dale of Cawsalta, K470 of the Royal Canadian Mounted Police. True to the tradition of the Mounties, he got his man.

In spite of the inborn scenting ability of a dog, it sometimes requires as long as a year and a half to train it to be a good tracker. In police work, it must learn to pick up a scent without the aid of an odor clue, for few criminals are sufficiently obliging to leave a cap or a handkerchief at the scene of the crime.

If it is known that a thief has entered a house

through a window, the dog is given a sniff of the sill. The dog then follows that specific odor and as long as the smell remains clear, there is no confusion. When Dale of Cawsalta was brought in to trail the lost child, he had one of her sweaters as a starting clue. It took him two hours to trace out that single odor from among the myriad others left by some hundred searchers, but once he was able to track it beyond the trampled area, he discovered the missing child within a very few minutes.

When there is no scent clue, the dog must learn to differentiate between odors that are natural to a given locality and the one scent that is alien to it. The smell of another dog did not belong among chinchilla rabbit hutches, and Wigger was keenly aware of it. Chief, the police dog, had been on the Force long enough to realize that the odor of illicit whisky is not usually found in a garbage dump. Neither does a coat button belong in open fields even though buried under snow.

One dog nosed out a lost wallet from beneath freshly plowed clods of earth. Wallets do not grow out of plowed ground; it was an alien scent and that was sufficient to attract the dog's attention. When the wind blew away three dollars that a woman had put in a milk pail, Dale found them almost immediately by the same process of scent elimination.

"This," says the nose of the dog, "belongs here —and this—and this—but not this. Here is a different smell, a strange smell. This is the one to follow."

With humans, the eyes perform the same function. Viewing the scene of a crime, police are continually alert to any object which is misplaced or has no reason for being there. The stub of a cigarette of a brand not smoked by anyone in the house is an important clue. A picture hanging crooked on a wall in an otherwise orderly room will start the police asking questions. So will a clump of mud that is different from the ground around that locality. Months of schooling and long years of experience are required to train a human law officer to such sharpness of perception. It takes about eighteen months for a dog. After that, the dog must work on his own, just as a man cannot keep running to his superiors for help. Initiative is essential to the successful solving of a crime and initiative is a factor of intelligence.

"The dogs on the Force," declare their handlers, "know nearly everything we say to them, and are sometimes smarter than we are."

"Dogs cannot reason," insist the majority of animal psychologists, "and without reason there can be no intelligence."

However, for the bewildered observer standing on the sidelines of this verbal battle between experts, there is the dog's record of achievement. This record is so impressive that more and more officials are enlisting the aid of dogs both as prison guards and in crime prevention.

After all, Egon of the Mounties forced a confession from a moonshiner by staring at him accusingly. And that in any man's language is known as "cracking a case."

5

Pegasus Without Wings

The stony ground of the hill in the middle of the desert had known the tread of His feet, the bushes had heard Him say, "Blessed are the meek . . . ."

There were no meek now to bless. The burning valley below was filled with the terrible and the proud. Knights in heavy armor, which the sun turned into bake ovens, were charging across the valley in a cloud of choking dust. Another cloud raced down to meet them. In its midst were Saracens, burnooses flying, steel helmets swathed in protecting folds of cloth, scimitars flashing like mirrors in the aching light.

The Crusaders on their great, armored chargers, braced themselves to meet the first shock of that vast, thundering wave, but it did not break upon them. It parted and swept around to cut off the mounted knights from the rest of the army, to attack from the rear; to separate French banner from English banner and, having separated them, to engage them in isolated groups. The long swords of the Christians, those swords that the Pope, himself, had blessed, came down upon the foe shining bright. When they were lifted again, they were blood red. Hour after hour the knights fought, knowing as they stood and died that they had been out-maneuvered by the lighter cavalry of the Infidels.

Viewing such a battle, the attention of the

observer naturally would be upon the men. The horses would be either ignored or taken for granted. But remove the horses and the scene would vanish. One cannot imagine a knight clanking along on foot, nor can one visualize the Saracens sweeping down on asses or camels. Neither animal has the courage nor the spirit for war.

Lacking the horse, there would have been no knights and hence no Crusades, as there would have been no Mongol invasion. While both of these great movements brought terror and death, they also opened new trade routes and introduced civilization into Europe, for then the culture of the world was centered in the East, at the courts of the Persian Shahs, in the tents of the Saracens, in the palaces of Genghis Khan. The Christians brought home more than jewel-hued rugs, delicate silks, peacock feathers, and carved ivory. They brought a desire for luxury and ease that had not been known since the fall of Rome.

All this was made possible because of the horse.

In America, the descendants of those few horses abandoned by the Conquistadores, changed the plains Indians from half-starved savages into great nations. Mounted, such tribes as the Sioux and the Comanche could follow the game trails, eat, and grow strong. Horses pulled the covered wagons in which men pioneered the West, horses carried the soldiers and scouts. Without the horse, there could have been no great cattle empires— and no cowboys.

The horse relieved man of the burdens he had always had to pack upon his own back. It enabled him to plow more land and so produce more food. Its greatest gift, however, was mobility. By carrying man swiftly from one place to another, the horse helped him to increase his area of activity and speed up the interchange of knowledge. Take away the horse and history would have to be rewritten. The chronology of civilization would be set back thousands of years.

From the time the first caveman mounted a wild pony, the human race has depended upon the horse as it has no other animal, save those which it killed for food—and often the horse served to assuage man's ever-present hunger. Yet the horse has been constantly overworked, beaten, and starved. The wonder of it is that instead of coming to hate the sight of a human being, horses have often strained every nerve and sinew not only to serve their masters but to bring them fame and fortune.

When Stephen C. Phillips sold Sleepy Tom, he did not realize he was sending him into brutal slavery. The horse, young then, had proved a disappointment. The blood of the great American thoroughbreds, Eclipse and Messenger, was in his veins, but Sleepy Tom showed none of their spirit and speed. In fact, the drowsy way he moved had given him his name.

Years later, after passing through many hands, he came back into Phillips' possession. It was not easy for the man to recognize in this miserable bag of bones the colt he had once owned. Compassion for the mistreated animal impelled Phillips to purchase him and turn him out to graze in lush pasture to regain his health and strength. Then quite by accident, Phillips discovered the horse's one talent—Sleepy Tom was a natural pacer.

At the time, fortunes were being made by trotters and pacers for harness racing was even more popular than it is today. So began the training of the horse for his new career.

To quote one of his biographers, Sleepy Tom was "the laughing stock of the crowd" when he first appeared on the track that memorable day in Ohio, but as the watchers saw the horse pull away from his competitors, his long, strong legs not once breaking their stride, laughter died into silence.

The pacing gait is not as dramatic as the trot. In fact, pacers have been jokingly dubbed "side wheelers." However, in a perfect pacing horse there is an hypnotic rhythm of motion that is beautiful to see. Sleepy Tom had that rhythm and he had more, stamina and speed. As he swept around the course to an easy victory, the crowd stood awed. They were witnessing a miracle and they knew it.

Sleepy Tom was running stone blind. The brutal treatment he had received from his previous owners had deprived him of his sight.

Keen though the scent and hearing may be in

a horse, its eyes are its most remarkable asset. Authorities who firmly state that most animals are color blind hesitate when it comes to the horse. "We are not sure," they say. "It may see color. Unfortunately, we cannot ask it."

However, it is known that the horse, like humans, has binocular vision. Unlike humans, each of its eyes sees a separate scene, together they cover a vast panorama. Theirs is a wide screen to our narrow one.

To bring objects into focus, the human eye expands and contracts. This the horse's eye cannot do, but it makes up for the deficiency by being set in a kind of bone ramp. The position is functionally perfect for it, especially in its wild state. By means of this slight upward tilt, it can see both the grass upon which it is browsing, and a potential enemy upon the horizon. It can see everything around it except that which is directly behind.

For example, one eye of a racing horse would

see the crowd lining the rail and filling the grandstand, while the other eye would be observing
the back stretch and the landscape beyond. At
the same time, the other horses coming up from
both sides would be well within the sweeping
range of its sight. Thus, because of the magnificent scope of its vision, the horse depends upon
its eyes as much as a human and far more than
a dog.

Imagine then Sleepy Tom pacing over the
course firmly, surely, swiftly—going forward into
total darkness.

The question as to whether or not horses possess intelligence must be asked again here. If, as
many authorities assert, horses act simply upon
instinct plus training, if they cannot understand
what man wishes them to do except by the appli-
cation of a long series of rewards and punish-
ments, then what of this blind horse that ran
solely upon the assurance, the confidence he
gained from his master's touch upon the reins, his

master's voice giving him orders that he instantly and unhesitatingly obeyed? Yet how could he have obeyed if he had not the ability to understand? No amount of training can include all the situations that arise during a race.

Sleepy Tom was not finding his way over the track by some sixth sense. His dependence upon his master was proved when, during one race, a mishap upset the two-wheel cart and Phillips was thrown out. Instantly, the horse stopped, nor would he move until his owner, badly shaken but otherwise unhurt, came back to speak to him and lead him away.

It would have been a marvel if Sleepy Tom could have run across a familiar pasture. As it was, he not only won race after race, he set a new world's record of a mile in 2:22½ minutes. This, it must be remembered, was not at a gallop, it was at a controlled, steady pace without once breaking the rhythm of the gait. Nor was this all. When he was thirteen years old, he lowered his own record to 2:12¼ minutes. Running neck and neck with him was the great pacer, Mattie Hunter. Mattie could see, Sleepy Tom could not, yet he nosed her out just as they crossed the finish line.

In all the scenes of equine achievement none is so thrilling as that of this horse coming down the last stretch, running in blind darkness to a glorious, a miraculous victory.

As with all animals, horses have a habit of blithely disproving every statement made about them by experts. Perhaps that is why the experts themselves cannot agree. There are those who claim that some horses are as loyal to their masters as a dog. An equal number as vehemently declare that the horse does not have enough brains to be loyal, that while it will eagerly greet the person who pets and feeds it, when taken to another place, it quickly forgets. It is a case of "out of sight, out of mind," if a horse can be said to have a mind.

Well, there is Snow Man. Snow Man is a jumper.

When one thinks of a jumper, there arises the image of a long-limbed thoroughbred, neck out-thrust, eyes flashing, spurning the earth in one magnificent leap like Pegasus without wings.

Andante, three times winner of "the horse of the year," would have fitted into that mental picture. So would the great Diamant, and the beautiful First Chance, famed jumpers all. Yet they were beaten by Snow Man, a broken-down plug so big and heavy it was obvious he must have Percheron blood in him, though what the rest of him was no one could tell.

Snow Man is another horse that had no cause to love humanity. Overworked, underfed, he could not even be sold at auction. He was thrown in with some fifteen other decrepit horses whose fate was to become dog food.

Harry De Leyer of Long Island, New York, saw Snow Man one bleak February day as the horse was being shoved into an already jammed truck. Sheer pity caused De Leyer to buy him for seventy dollars, though afterward he said it was the indomitable gleam in the big horse's eyes that attracted him. Certainly it was not Snow Man's appearance. He was so covered with filth that it took five washings to get him clean. The sores that marked his skin gradually healed, but nothing could eradicate the deep grooves made by the plow harness he had worn so long.

If De Leyer hoped that he could use the horse at the Knox School for Girls where he was riding master, he met with disappointment. Snow Man was much too heavy hoofed for a young ladies' seminary. Finally, De Leyer sold him for a hundred and forty dollars to a doctor who lived on the other side of town.

At the doctor's, the horse was as well treated as he had been at the De Leyers'. According to those experts who disclaim the loyalty of the horse, Snow Man should have promptly forgotten the man who had saved him from becoming Fido's dinner. Instead, the big horse jumped the doctor's fence and returned to his benefactor. De Leyer, of course, took him back to his new owner. The doctor added another bar to the fence. Snow Man jumped that, and again showed up at the De Leyers', only to be again returned. This went on for some time. Higher and higher grew that fence, and higher and higher Snow Man jumped to clear it. Finally, De Leyer gave in, handed the purchase

price to the doctor and put the horse out to pasture. Only then did he realize that he owned a natural jumper.

No one can teach a horse to jump. Either the ability is born in it, or it is not. All a trainer can do is to improve its technique, and this De Leyer set out to accomplish with Snow Man. Immediately the big, white plug started falling over his own hoofs. He could not clear a three-foot bar. De Leyer was about to give up when it apparently dawned on the horse what his master wanted— not plowing, *jumping*. From then on, Snow Man jumped over everything that was put in his way. Moreover, he did what few horses will do, jumped on command without a rider to guide him.

Within a few years, Snow Man had won three of the most coveted open jumping titles in the horse world, the Professional Horseman's Association Champion, the American Horse Shows Association High Score Award, and the National Championship. He had shown at such aristocratic meets as Sands Point, Piping Rock, and Madison Square Garden, had won thousands in prize money, and a man had offered to buy him for a hundred thousand dollars, an offer which De Leyer refused.

From intended dog meat to stardom, from seventy dollars to a hundred thousand is a long jump, but it has been made with equal success by other horses. What is memorable in Snow Man is not his ring record or his financial worth, it is the love and loyalty he showed to the first human being who had ever been kind to him. For love and loyalty are impossible without memory, and conscious, not instinctive, memory is said to be an aspect of intelligence.

Snow Man's life reads like a fairy tale, yet equine history is filled with such stories. Old horses, destined for the butcher's or the glue factory, become blue ribbon champions under the magic wand of understanding and kindness. Rejected and despised foals grow up to step into the spotlight and earn fabulous fortunes.

The record of Kincsem is merely one example of the ever recurring Cinderella theme in the horse world, and were this all, the tale would not be worth retelling. But Kincsem seemed fated to disprove every law in the book compiled by horse experts.

Although a thoroughbred, the little Hungarian-born foal was the ugliest creature one could imagine. She had legs like stilts and a tail that resembled an old broom. Skinny fore and aft, she was pot-bellied in the middle, and on top of that, she was lop-eared. Why her owner named her Kincsem is a mystery. It may be that he called her "Treasure" in mocking jest. Having done so, he forgot about her—until one moonless night a gypsy crept into the stable and stole the little filly.

The thief was traced to his camp, and there beside the fire, ringed by the gaily painted gypsy wagons drawn up under the trees, Kincsem's owner faced the horse stealer more in bewilderment than in anger. "My stables are filled with magnificent horses," he said. "You could have taken any one of them. Why did you choose that ugly little thing?"

"Because," said the gypsy, "she will be the greatest of them all."

Kincsem's owner scoffed, but he could not rid himself of the thought that gypsies are noted for their second sight. Even as he laughed at his own gullibility, he put Kincsem in training. A year later he entered her in her first race, but he thought so little of her that he did not bother to attend the meet to see how she ran.

Kincsem ran twelve lengths ahead of the field.

When she beat the finest thoroughbreds Germany could produce, the racing world began to take notice of this ungainly young mare. But it was not until she appeared at a race in Budapest that Kincsem revealed that trait which was to bring Europe in general, and her riders in particular, to the verge of a nervous breakdown.

All authorities agree that with a horse, to run is as instinctive as to breathe. Flight has been its principal means of survival through the millions of years of its existence. When it comes to track racing, however, the experts break up into three opposing groups.

Group A claims that competitive racing is not natural to a horse, therefore it has to be forced to run. Eddie Arcaro, the world-famous jockey, admits that most horses have little interest in winning and have to be urged on by their riders.

Group B holds that while a horse may be nervous and uncertain at first when faced by a strange track and a tumultuous crowd, once it has known the excitement of a race, it is eager to experience it again. Here these experts are careful to explain that horses cannot know what a race means in human terms. They simply like to run and to try to take the lead. Some have been known to nip viciously at a rival horse challenging their position in the race.

On the other hand, Group C declares that the actions of a horse depend upon whether it is the dominant or recessive type. It has long been known that horses are social snobs. The observance of precedent is far more rigidly enforced in the equine world than in the world of humans. The leader of a herd always drinks first at a stream, takes the best plot of grass, and goes through an open gate ahead of the others. After it come the runners up, the would-be leaders who did not quite make the grade. These are the dominant type. Next are the ones who would like to lead but have not enough courage to fight for it. After them, at the bottom of the social list, are those who have no ambition at all and are content to follow. These are the recessive type.

The fearful and the meek, say the experts of Group C, do not dare go ahead of their social superiors. If they attempt to thrust in where they do not belong, they are soundly bitten and kicked. This equine protocol is observed on the race course just as it is out on the range or in a pasture. If a race horse does not want to run, it may be the recessive type. In this case, its apparent disinterest and laziness would be actually a reluctance to pass the dominant horses on the track for fear of instant reprisal. Of course, the dominant type in a race would be eager to run, and it would be natural for them to fight for leadership just as they do in a wild herd.

It would be interesting to know what these three groups of experts would say about Kincsem. During her first racing year, she got away from the barrier with the rest of the horses, took the lead and kept it. Then suddenly in her second year, she began to show less and less interest as she came to the post. In the Budapest race, while the other horses were being jockeyed into position, Kincsem was grazing on a bit of grass beside the track; her rider could do nothing with her. Assistants came to his aid but "Treasure" refused to be coaxed, pulled, or pushed. Finally

the starter had to send off the rest without her. Kincsem, grass still dribbling out of her mouth, looked mildly after them—and began to run. She caught up with them at the stretch and surged ahead to an easy victory.

Kincsem's approach to the post would have shamed a milk wagon plug. Where the proud thoroughbreds paced and pranced, she plodded. Having arrived at the starting line, she just stood there, tail drooping, head down. In race after race she was left behind, while every track fan in Europe held his breath and chewed his nails. Yet somehow she always managed to win. In fact, she won so consistently that at last bookmakers refused to give odds on her.

When she had conquered all the continent's best racers, she was taken to England to compete against the Prince of Wales's famous horse, Pageant, for the Goodwood Cup. There, soothed by the excited roar of a record crowd, Kincsem went to sleep at the post. Pageant was far out in front before she even woke up. Looking slightly flustered, she started after him. When she crossed the finish line, she was three lengths ahead.

The Prince of Wales offered a fortune for her, but her owner did not dare sell his nation's "Treasure." If he had, he would have been banished from Hungary.

At home, in a palace made into a stable, Kincsem regularly held court, delicately nibbling hay while thousands of Hungarians waited in line just to pass by her stall. She died at the age of fourteen and every paper in Hungary bordered the news in black as though she were royalty. Noble and commoner mourned the passing of the horse whose future the gypsy thief had so accurately foretold.

During her career, Kincsem raced fifty-four times, and won fifty-four times. She was indeed the greatest of them all. She was also a large headache to her adoring public, and she is still a headache to the horse experts.

Did Kincsem want to race or did she not? Was she the dominant or the recessive type? Who knows? As the authorities would say, "Unfortunately, we cannot ask her."

6

Beyond Fear

The recorded history of war dogs goes back to
700 B.C., but the use of dogs in battle is undoubtedly much older. In western Europe, the Romans
were the first to form their version of the K-9
Corps when they ringed their cities with mastiffs
to act as sentries. In the Middle Ages, dogs wore
armor like their master-knights, and carried upon
their breastplates their owners' coats-of-arms.

Some of these dogs were mastiffs, but many of them were greyhounds, only then they were called "gaze hounds," because they found their quarry by sight rather than scent or sound.

Spiked iron collars for guard and sentry dogs as a protection against wild animals was recommended by Varo, a Roman writer, but it took the Gauls to improve upon the idea. They fastened knives to their dogs' collars and sent them against the enemy. As the dogs ran wild among the cavalry, the knives in their collars sliced through leg tendons, disabling the horses and causing panic and rout. In Shakespeare's *Julius Caesar,* when Antony says, "Cry, Havoc! and let slip the dogs of war," it was not merely a pretty figure of speech. For thousands of years, dogs have accompanied men into battle, just as did Andreas von Wiede-Hurst, better known to the Marines of M Company as Andy.

Andy was a thoroughbred Doberman pinscher. Because of the proud way he walked, he was nicknamed "Gentleman Jim," and he was a gentleman in every sense of the word. There was a gaiety about him combined with absolute dependability. Children and puppies could maul him, but he tolerated no nonsense from any male, dog or man, that dared challenge his rights. When he became a Marine, he transferred his unswerving loyalty and obedience from his owner, Theodore Andrea Wiedeman, of Norristown, Pennsylvania, to his two handlers, PFC Robert E. Lansley, of Syracuse, New York, and PFC Jack Mahoney, of Clinton, Connecticut. He was with them when they were sent across the Pacific to Bougainville.

There is nothing more beautiful than a jungle-covered, coral-ringed island lying on the blue, swelling breast of the ocean. Here the voice of the sea is answered by the rustling of the trees in the trade winds. The jewel-colored plumage of parakeets in the branches is matched by the iridescence of fishes in the sapphire water where diamond sparks of light wink back at the sun.

This was what the Marines saw from their landing boats. What they heard was the boom of hidden Japanese batteries that turned the golden beaches into a place of death. In one of the boats were the members of the K-9 Corps and their handlers. Kneeling beside the dogs, the men sought with hand and voice to quiet the fear of their four-footed companions.

But why were the dogs afraid? During their training they had become accustomed to all types of shellfire. The Messenger dogs had small mines blown up behind them as they raced across broken fields from one handler to another. So close had those explosions been that the dirt had sprayed over them. The Scout dogs had been sent once a week to the demolition range. There, with their handlers, they had learned to crawl on their bellies while officers hurled half-pound blocks of TNT around them. There could have been no difference even to a dog's keen ears between the sound of a Japanese battery and an American

one. None of their five senses could have told them that this was a real, not a sham, battle in which they were about to take part. Nor could they have been frightened by the thought of approaching danger and possible death. An animal has no understanding of death until it is upon him. On this point all the authorities agree. Still the dogs were afraid.

They were afraid because their human companions were afraid. Fear was in the air. It was contagious and the dogs caught it. So in this Pacific amphibian assault upon the island of Bougainville, Andy and his K-9 companions had to be comforted by their handlers. Once they hit the beach and went into action, they were beyond fear. There was no time for personal emotion in either men or dogs. Andy and his human companions, Lansley and Mahoney, were sent forward almost at once upon patrol duty.

The invasion had caught the Japanese by surprise. Reinforcements would have to be rushed to the front. This the Americans knew. They also knew that there were two trails by which those reinforcements could come, the Numa-Numa and the Piva. As the Piva crossed the Numa-Numa, this trail was chosen for some two hundred and fifty Marines to patrol. Up from the beaches they went toward the mountains, with Andy in the lead.

Psychologists say that in a human the ability to quickly orient to unfamiliar situations and surroundings is a sign of high intelligence. What then of a dog? Within two hours after landing, Andy was skillfully guiding the Marines through a jungle so dense that the men often had to carve a path out of the tangled green mass.

Back in the States, Andy had been trained to work in swamps and thick brush in preparation for combat duty in the tropics, but American swamps are not jungles. They do not look or sound or smell the same. Andy's color blindness prevented him from seeing the green of the living walls that closed them in. To him, this strange new world was composed of varying shades of gray. The silver-gold of a shaft of sunlight, slipping in through a break in the dense foliage overhead, was merely a brighter spot that felt hot when he passed through it.

To the Marines moving forward with tense, alert caution, the jungle was a place of silence, a silence disturbed rather than broken by the constant hum of insects that shifted and drifted around them like an invisible curtain.

To Andy, the jungle was excitingly noisy. His ears reported the rustle of a leaf far above, the scuttle of an unseen beetle in the grass beneath, the dry, bursting sound a bud makes when it opens, the plop of seeds dropping like falling pebbles.

It was his nose though more than any of his other senses that told him this was unfamiliar country. The odor of a jungle is compounded largely of decaying vegetation and damp, moldy earth, layer upon layer of rotting trees, brush, and vines. This is obvious even to human nostrils, but Andy caught the whiff of minute gases given off by this decay. Just by scent he could tell the difference between a growing bush and a dead one. To him, a wet stone did not smell the same as a dry one.

Andy, prancing some twenty-five yards ahead of the patrol, was having the time of his life. He caught no scent of fear from the men following him because they were too keyed up to be afraid. He did not know that this dense mass of trees and vines could conceal a Japanese sniper or an enemy battery—not until the odor came down to him on the wind. He knew that smell. In the training camps at home, almond-eyed men who gave off just such a scent had made his life miserable by unexpectedly leaping from hiding, shouting at him and waving pieces of cloth or knives under his nose. These were the loyal Japanese who proudly bore the scars of many a dog's teeth in the performance of their duty. That duty was to acquaint the K-9 Corps with the smell, sight, and sound of the enemy. In the Service, they were known as "aggravators." Andy had good reason to dislike these aggravators. The instant he scented them, he knew it was his job to give warning.

Early in the training period, handlers found that some dogs were difficult to "read," some "easy." Andy was easy. There was no mistaking the hackles that rose on the back of his neck, nor was there any uncertainty as to the location of the enemy. Andy's nose pointed directly toward a mango tree. Though the Marines could see only dense foliage, they did not hesitate to act on Andy's information. The instant he halted rigid, they hit the ground—a split second ahead of an explosion of machine-gun fire from a concealed battery.

Three times Andy alerted the men on that long jungle trek. Because of him, a Japanese sniper, an enemy patrol, and another camouflaged battery were wiped out. Two hundred and fifty Marines went into that jungle. Thanks to Andy of the K-9 Corps, two hundred and fifty Marines came out.

The heroism of Scout, Sentry, and Red Cross dogs was more than matched by the Messengers. The training of these dogs was entirely different from that of other branches of the Service. From the start each dog was assigned to two handlers. Both of the men had to win the dog's friendship in order to inspire in him an affectionate loyalty and a desire to seek out the one that, at the moment, was absent. The key word was "Report." One handler would slip a piece of paper into a metal tube or a leather pouch, pat the dog and say, "Report," whereupon the dog would run to the other handler. At first, the two men stood about twenty feet apart. Gradually, the distance was increased to over a mile. Once the dog knew what was expected of him, he was never sent over the same route twice. Other men were stationed along his course to try to distract his attention, for too often in the Pacific theater of war, the Japs, seeing a K-9 Messenger, would attempt to coax him over to them, calling, "Doggie, Doggie," in both English and Japanese. So the dog had to learn to ignore all voices and all tempting bits of food that, in enemy hands, might be poisoned. Also he had to learn that he could not pause to investigate fascinating scents on the way. Often the life of a Company depended upon the speed

and courage of a Messenger dog, as it did with Sandy.

This was on the island of New Britain just east of New Guinea. The Marines had been sent there with orders to seize two Jap landing fields. On paper, the orders looked simple. In reality they were difficult and dangerous for these landing strips were guarded by pillboxes that had to be blasted out before the Marines could advance. Walkie-talkies connected forward units with the main body and they worked efficiently until a tropical storm put them out of commission.

Fortunately, Sandy was there with one of his handlers, Sergeant Brown. The enemy barrage that pinned down the Marines in mud did not bother Sandy. Shellfire had never bothered this four-year-old German shepherd, and he was impatient for action. He enjoyed his work. It was exciting to zigzag between the hail of bullets, to race over and around all sorts of obstacles, for at the end of the run a second friend was waiting to pat him and praise him for a job well done.

Sandy quivered with eagerness when Sergeant Brown slipped the message into the pouch under his neck, a message giving the position of the pillboxes along with an urgent request that the artillery do something about them. For an instant, Brown stroked the dog, then he said, "Report!" That was all Sandy needed. The enemy saw him streak away and tried to shoot him, but in the streaming rain and thick brush, he made a difficult target. Then, too, he ran crouched so close to the ground and swerved so constantly there was little chance of getting him even with a machine gun.

Out of firing range, Sandy put on more speed. He plunged through tall Kunai grass until he came to a river. The river was swollen by the deluge from the sullen skies. Logs swept by on its crest. A native chicken coop disintegrated practically under Sandy's nose. Anyone looking at that raging flood might have questioned the dog's chances of getting through, but Sandy did not stop to question. He simply jumped in and swam to the opposite shore. Somewhere back behind the lines, his good friend, Sergeant Sheldon, was waiting for him and Sandy was not going to disappoint him. Only Sheldon was not waiting for him. He had no way of learning that the dog had been sent back. Had he known, he would have been a worried man for he was not in the same place Sandy had left him. He had been moved to another position along the line.

Experts say that a dog returns to his home or master by utilizing his powers of scent and sight. If taken in a car to another locality, he can find his way back by remembering details of the landscape which humans ignore. This, of course, infers that dogs have excellent sight, yet these same authorities declare that a dog's vision is about forty percent *less* than that of a man, that due to the shape of his eyes he is afflicted with astigmatism, and that his field of vision is foreshortened. In a room, for example, the ceiling appears to a dog to curve down into the back wall. Tests have shown that a dog can make out forms a little more than half a mile away, but the dogs that were tested had exceptionally keen sight. The average dog's limit of vision is around a quarter of a mile.

However, in this instance, it would have been impossible for Sandy, carrying the vital message from the pinned-down Marines, to have followed the trail by sight. To begin with, he had been brought up to the front on foot, and half the way he could not see over the Kunai grass that, in places, grew as tall as a man. This grass would have effectively prevented him from memorizing details of the landscape. Neither could Sandy have followed the trail by scent because the pouring rain had wiped it out. Besides, both sight-memory and trail-scent would have been useless, for Sandy's other handler was no longer where the dog had left him.

In spite of all this, Sandy set a beeline course to where his friend *had been transferred*. The first that Sheldon knew of the dog's presence was when sixty pounds of German shepherd leaped the barbed wire entanglement and fell with tail-wagging joy upon him, where he was crouching in a foxhole.

How did Sandy find his way? No one knows, but the message from the front was delivered, artillery went into action, the pillboxes were demolished, and the Marines moved in to take the landing field from the enemy.

That same enemy, K-9 Scout Wolf came to know only too well. He met them in the Philippines. There he brilliantly guided many patrols, but it was in the Corabello Mountains that this big German shepherd showed the greatness that was in him.

Wolf was leading an infantry patrol up toward Belete Pass, a strategic point in the area. The patrol was advancing with the utmost caution, for

the rugged, jungle-covered mountains could conceal a regiment. Suddenly Wolf halted and
pointed toward a hill about a hundred and fifty
yards ahead. The scent of the enemy had come
to him through the myriad odors of trees, flower-
ing shrubs and vines that mantled the mountain-
side. The soldiers promptly took cover and
opened fire. They were answered by the roar of
Japanese guns from the exact spot Wolf had
indicated.

As the battle raged on, it slowly dawned on the Americans that they were not only outnumbered, they were being surrounded. Shells were ripping up the ground all about them. The air was filled with splinters of shrapnel. Wolf was struck by some of these flying fragments. The men did not know he was wounded. The dog showed no sign of pain, not a whimper escaped him. K-9 Scouts were trained to be silent on duty, but that training did not include being pierced by deadly shell splinters. Yet Wolf seemed to know that a sound from him might mean death to the men. Besides, they were depending upon him, and upon him alone. Ignoring his own agony, he concentrated all his attention upon the task of finding a way of escape before the jaws of the enemy trap completely closed.

Again and again Wolf alerted the American patrol just in time to avoid a detachment of Japanese. Back and forth they wove across the shoulder of the mountain, the men following the dog, trusting him. At last, Wolf discovered a route of retreat. He led his human companions all the way down the mountain and back to the command post. Not until he had safely delivered them did he reveal his pain. The men, stunned by the realization that he had been wounded, rushed him to the hospital. There they waited hoping, praying, through the long emergency operation that followed. They knew that they owed their lives to this dog. When they learned that Wolf had given his own life to save theirs, these battle-hardened soldiers openly wept.

The honor roll of the K-9 Corps is long and contains such illustrious names as Caeser, Duke, Lady, Dick, and Jack.

Jack, a Belgian shepherd Messenger dog, was given a citation by General Holcomb for "outstanding performance of duty in combat." It was even rumored that he was to be advanced to sergeant. In a fine state of dismay, the dog's handler, PFC Gordon J. Wortman, wrote to his family, "That's really going to be tough. How can I give orders to a dog when he has a higher rating than I do?"

Yet at first there was a strong prejudice against the members of the K-9 Corps. Who wanted or needed dogs in this age of mechanization? Officers were reluctant to use them, and their handlers had to plead for them to be given a chance. Once the dogs had proved what they could do, urgent demands for more and more dogs deluged Headquarters.

The 28th Infantry Scout Dog Platoon is an example of K-9 efficiency. In more than *eight hundred patrols* led by dogs, not a single man was lost.

This is an astounding record. One is tempted to say, "Who cares how they did it as long as so many lives were saved?" Such an attitude may be sufficient for past events, but what of the future?

When Andy, on Bougainville, scented two

concealed batteries, one on each side of the Piva trail, he could not say, "Look, fellows, the Japs have us in a cross fire," yet it was part of his duty to relay that information to the men following him. He did it by pointing first to one hidden battery, then whirling and pointing to the other.

If it can be proved that animals are intelligent, then perhaps some better form of communication can be established between us and them.

Take the case of Sandy's trailing ability. It is a well-known fact that some dogs can be lost by simply going around a couple of blocks. It is equally well-known that dogs have found their way back over thousands of miles of unknown territory. Is the difference in the dogs, or is it in the desire, the passionate wish to return to a beloved home or master? Does this passionate wish supply the energy to activate some kind of a built-in radio beam whereby the dog can get a "fix" on his destination regardless of the distance that lies between?

With Wolf, what prevented him from showing that he was mortally wounded? Was it instinct plus training; or was it the knowledge that absolute silence was essential to the safety of the patrol surrounded by an enemy covering every inch of ground in search of them?

These are some of the questions experts are asking. They are important questions, and we must find the answers, for we may be making the grave mistake of underrating these animals with which mankind has been associated for thousands of years.

7

Enter—A Star!

The time was the first century A.D., the place, the ancient city of Antioch. The Circus was crowded to its capacity. Every seat in the grandstand was filled with men in handsome togas and women in flowing gowns, caught at the waist by gold and jeweled belts. In his box sat the Roman Consul, banked by legionary standards and surrounded by his family and officials. Below him spread the vast oblong arena covered with white sand. Down the center ran the *spina,* a decorated stone wall some five feet high, the equivalent of the inner rail of the modern race track. Around this the chariot races were run. The track was wide enough for four chariots abreast with from four to six horses harnessed to each chariot.

The citizens of Antioch, however, had not paid their money to view a race. They had come to witness a catastrophe, and they were ready to take the place apart should they be disappointed. Not to disappoint them, the chariot in the outer lane was started first, the one next to the *spina* last. The result was that all sixteen to twenty-four horses reached the first turn at the same time in a crashing mass of chariots, animals, and men. The horses that could still stand went on with the race regardless of whether their driver was in the chariot, or even if there was a chariot. They might be dragging two wheels or merely a length of harness; still they ran. Seven times they circled that track before they were stopped. Horses and men struggling up out of a tangle of splintered wood and torn reins were knocked down again and trampled. Horses rearing, slashing each other with their hoofs; horses racing neck and neck raked each other with snapping teeth. It was all very colorful, exciting, and brutal.

This is the scene that is the highlight of General Lew Wallace's immortal novel. In fact, without the chariot race there would be no *Ben Hur,* at least for motion pictures. The story has been filmed many times, the last filming being made in Italy. When Glen Randall, one of Hollywood's most successful horse trainers, was asked to go abroad to school the horses for the race, he knew that he was being handed a large order.

The picture version was supposed to follow the ancient Roman one as closely as possible, but even for a motion picture striving for realism, one could not wantonly kill or maim valuable animals, not to mention the charioteers. The

scenes would have to be tricked. This meant training the animals for individual shots, some to rear, some to fall, some to stage a mock fight. It meant obtaining horses that were big and strong enough to run that grueling race, beautiful enough to be photogenic, and intelligent enough to be taught.

Glen Randall found what he wanted in the Lipizzans. This breed is part Arabian, it has the Arabian horse's pride and grace of carriage, but it is taller and heavier. For centuries in Europe, Lipizzans have been the favorite horses of circus bareback riders. Lipizzans are also the horses most frequently used in dressage. In the horse world, the ability to learn the complicated routine of dressage, with its various gaits, dance steps and even leaps, is comparable to achieving a doctor's degree among humans. Few horses can make the grade.

Many trainers and animal psychologists insist that no animal understands human speech. It grasps the intent of what is said through voice inflection and gestures, yet when Glen Randall started to train his Lipizzans, he discovered that they did not understand him, regardless of how he pitched his voice and waved his arms. Some of the horses knew only Sicilian, some Yugoslavian, none had been taught English. Randall had to teach them to recognize commands in his own language, not only because he did not have time to learn theirs but because the men who would drive them would be English-speaking actors.

In five months these horses had to be ready to go before the camera—five months in which to become familiar with a new vocabulary, to master their separate acting roles, to become accustomed to all the strange sights, sounds, and smells of a foreign country, to the roars of the crowd before which they would race, as well as to the lights and confusion of a motion picture set.

Can this ability to learn, and learn with

amazing speed, be considered a mark of intelligence? "Of course," said Glen Randall. "If a trainer didn't think horses were intelligent, he couldn't teach them."

Though Randall has schooled hundreds of horses to work before the cameras, one horse, for him, stands out as the most intelligent of all. That one is Trigger, Roy Rogers' "Golden Palomino." Trigger is a "liberty horse," that is he works without reins or physical contact of any kind. In Randall's opinion, Trigger can do anything that any picture horse can do or has ever done. Trigger responds to some sixty different commands given by voice or signals, and like all real actors, he loves to appear before both audience and camera.

When the Rogers Rodeo played in Madison Square Garden, New York, Trigger was impatiently waiting to go on long before Dale Evans and Roy Rogers had finished making up. Trigger is also alert to any variation that will improve his act. During one of his stage appearances, he discovered that when he blew into a microphone, fascinating noise came out. The audience loved it and from then on, Trigger saw to it that mike blowing was part of his routine. But he is firm in insisting that he receive the homage due a star of his magnitude. In New York, a big party was given for Dale, Roy, and members of the cast. In one corner of the huge ballroom Trigger had a place of his own, covered with imitation grass. Here he graciously received his fans, but if someone passing failed to pause and pat him, Trigger snorted loudly to attract attention.

In the twenty years that Trigger has been playing with Rogers, he has crossed and recrossed the United States more than thirty times. His foreign appearances have included Canada, the British Isles, South America, and Honolulu. He is a seasoned traveler, this horse of every small boy's dream; nothing ever bothers him. After an exhausting day jouncing over long, hot roads, he will appear at the theater or rodeo grounds as fresh as though he had been sleeping in a quiet, green pasture, and he can be counted on to go through his act without a single mistake. When one realizes that one of these tours includes as many as forty one-night stands, this is a record of which any actor could be proud.

At home, however, Trigger likes to play a few tricks. His favorite is one that he learned for a feature picture. The action required him to come charging out through an open door fighting. The scene was a huge success, but Trigger saw possibilities in it for his own use. Now, when someone opens his door quickly, he will come blasting out as though ready for a fight. Then, having scared the person out of his wits, Trigger stops and regards his victim with bright, amused eyes.

Before camera or audience though, play is forgotten. Trigger's millions of fans expect him to turn in a good performance and he never disappoints them, even when called upon to fight a mountain lion. Horses hate these big cats, as well they should. Millions of years ago, their ancestors equally hated the saber-toothed tiger. Here in this scene, Trigger had to face one of the deadly enemies of his race. Had he been governed solely by instinct, he would either have resorted to flight or turned on the cat with ripping hoofs and snapping teeth. Instead, he did what Glen Randall told him to do, just as every actor obeys his director. There was the mountain lion up on top of a rock, sunk back on its powerful haunches, ready to spring. Only a few feet below stood Trigger rearing, snorting, pawing, but not once moving out of camera range.

In choosing horses for picture work, Randall seeks intelligence first. "An intelligent horse looks like he has sense," he explained. "He has a broad, well-balanced head, alert ears, large bright eyes. Trouble is," he added with a touch of wry humor, "the smarter the horse, the smarter the trainer has to be."

On the other hand, Jay Barry, trainer of such famous horses as Gene Autry's Champion, and Champion, Jr., claims that the important quality in a horse is a good disposition. Champion, Jr. has it. To quote Barry, "He doesn't get excited about anything. You can take him into a hospital full of kids, and as long as he has enough room to move, he never bothers. One time, in a town in Iowa, I left Champ to eat lunch. When I came back, there were seven kids sitting on his back.

You'd be in plenty of trouble in a case like that if you had a bad horse."

Champ, Jr.'s ability to withstand the rigors of a tour of one-night stands amazes even his trainer. Sometimes they have had to drive seven hundred miles in a single day to meet engagements. Champ, Jr. travels in a thirty-five foot, air-conditioned trailer, and never becomes tired or cross as most horses do when being hauled from place to place, and he is always ready to perform.

He puts on quite a performance, too. Aside from doing the usual tricks of bowing, saying his prayers, and playing dead, Champ does several dance steps. His most spectacular act is jumping up on a baby grand piano. "It's easy to get a horse to jump," Barry said, "but they want to jump *over*. It's not easy to stop on top of a piano." Yet Champ, Jr. does it every time.

Getting a horse into a building is always difficult. Few people realize that horses need ramps to mount safely. Champion has had to become accustomed to steps, like humans. "But he has that kind of a disposition," said his trainer. "It's just as though he says, 'Wherever you go, I'll go too, if I have to walk a plank.' " Champ, Jr. has ridden on more than a hundred elevators. It is his trainer's ambition to have him go up an escalator. "He'd do it, too," he said. "Champ would ride it just as nice. You have no idea the things he's done."

It takes a good trouper to meet the hardships of around-the-world travel and remain cheerful. A serene disposition, as Jay Barry insists, is an important factor. Only once did Champ Jr. lose his temper. "That was when this fellow came on the stage disguised as a reindeer. Champ had a fit," Barry remembered humorously. "He ran the guy right off. We never did know whether Champ just didn't like reindeer or if he was afraid the reindeer might steal the show."

But Mr. Barry does not believe that a horse has either initiative or intelligence. "I don't recall," he said, "ever seeing a horse do anything on his own except eat and drink and open a gate. They hate everything you do except feed them. Let's face it."

Mr. Lee Duncan does not agree with this. "One of my best friends," he declared, "was pulled off his horse by a bull he was trying to rope. He was alone and badly hurt, but his horse stood over him for hours until he regained consciousness. No one taught the horse to do that. He could easily have run away, but he knew that his master needed him."

To Duncan, all animals are intelligent in a greater or lesser degree. He owns a number of beautiful horses, but he is not a horse trainer. He is the owner of the famous canine motion picture and television star, Rin Tin Tin.

The original Rin Tin Tin was not a dog. He was a man, a young Frenchman, and he pro- nounced his name *Ron-Tahn-Tahn*. Rin was very much in love with a beautiful girl called Nannette.

During World War I, the village in which they lived was bombed by the Germans. The lovers took refuge in a cellar. Everyone in the village was killed except these two. It was as though they had a charmed life. The story of their miraculous escape spread over France and small doll pins of the famous couple were made as good luck charms. Many of the Allied fliers wore them on their tunics when they went into combat. Captain Lee Duncan was one of those fliers.

When he acquired two German shepherd puppies during his stay in France, he remembered the story of the lovers and called the male puppy Rin Tin Tin. The dog grew up to become the first of the canine picture stars. There have been four Rin Tin Tins since that day in 1918. The last Rin has been on television for five years.

According to his owner-trainer, Rin is more camerawise than most human actors, and he has a natural sense of scene pacing. "One time on a set," Duncan said, "a little boy didn't open a door

fast enough, and Rin did it for him. I didn't teach
Rin to do that. Another time, the little boy was
saying his prayers and Rin got down and said
his prayers with him. I didn't teach him to do
that either. He was constantly doing things like
that by himself.

"Are dogs intelligent? Of course they are." Lee
Duncan paused and smiled reminiscently. "People often ask me if I don't think my Rin is the
greatest dog in the world. I tell them I don't. The

greatest dog in the world is the one *you* own, and don't you ever forget it."

Rin Tin Tin is not the only canine in Hollywood to wear the crown of stardom. There is Lassie. At the Desilu Studios, a special room is set aside where the famous star can relax between scenes.

It is difficult to say "he" when speaking of this dog because of its name, but Lassie is a male. A female collie cannot appear consistently before the camera. It is not that she has less intelligence and ability, it is because the females lose their hair during the summer and, with it, their beautiful neck ruff. Lassie has to work five days a week, every week, and there is no time to wait for the dog to grow new hair. To date, Lassie has made two hundred and sixteen television pictures.

This would be an exhausting schedule for anyone, but Lassie loves his work so much that he can scarcely wait to get to the studio, and when he thinks that he is being left out of the picture

for too many scenes, he begins to pace impatiently around the set and to make little protesting
sounds in the back of his throat. After all, he is
the main attraction. Were it not for Lassie, the
people playing with him would be out of work.

Weekends, this famous star relaxes at the ranch
of his owner-trainer, Rudd Weatherwax. Here
Lassie herds cows. He does not herd ducks. In
fact, he never had anything to do with ducks
until a flock of them were brought on the set one
morning.

The desire to chase anything that moves, from
automobiles to fowls, is instinctive in a dog, but
as soon as the cameras began to roll, Lassie ten-
derly shepherded those excitable, quacking ducks
through a gate as though he had been doing it all
his life. Then the director wanted the gate shut
behind them. This bit of business had not been
included in the rehearsal, yet Lassie went back
and closed the gate without an instant's hesitation.

According to Rudd Weatherwax, Lassie acts

on his own initiative about eighty percent of the time. "He's an actor, not a trick dog," Weatherwax explained. "A trick dog is one that is taught certain tricks and does them over and over. He never has to vary them. That's the kind you'll find in vaudeville. Lassie has to do something different each time."

Not long ago, Lassie was challenged by another star to prove which was more intelligent, the horse or the dog. The challenger was the famous and beautiful stallion, Fury. Unfortunately, prior picture engagements prevented both of them from making the test.

"If they had," said Ralph McCutcheon, "I would have put my money on Fury." This loyalty to the horse is understandable. Mr. McCutcheon is the owner-trainer of Fury.

There is an enthusiasm about Ralph McCutcheon that is contagious. His horses have caught it, all one hundred and four of them. When their trainer is in sight, they never take their bright, eager eyes off of him. The attraction is mutual. McCutcheon loves horses. "I like to show them off," he said, "the same way parents show off their children." He finds horses quick to learn and easy to train.

One of his equine actors is a gorgeous palomino named California. California can stage a terrific fight with another horse before the cameras, but the instant the scene is over, he is as gentle as a lamb. In one such combat, California gave such a magnificent performance that the spectators began to wonder if the stage fight would erupt into a real one, as it has many times with human actors. Instead, when the scene was over, California ambled across to a little girl standing on the sidelines, and playfully thrust his head under her arm.

It seems that not all horses lose control when they become excited, experts to the contrary. However, McCutcheon's horses are actors. With them, "The play's the thing." They do not need their trainer to tell them to stop acting when the scene is over.

There is only one real star though on the McCutcheon ranch. That star is Fury. Big, beautiful, and black, he takes direction better than the human actors appearing with him. In one television scene, Fury was required to come galloping out of his stall. This, in itself, is quite a feat. On a stage set, there is no room for a horse to change from a walk to a run, he has to go into a gallop from a standing start. Add to this the element of timing. Fury had to make his entrance at the exact instant one of the actors was speaking. The horse raced out on cue all right, but the man forgot his lines. Fury gave him a disgusted look and went back into his stall to be ready for a retake. McCutcheon did not have to tell him to do that, nor was he trained to do it. Fury knew that the scene had been ruined and would have to be shot again.

"I never fool my horses," McCutcheon said

emphatically. "I know one trainer who sticks pins in a horse to make him do a fast spurt of running before the camera. That I would never do. I tell the horse what I want and rehearse him a few times. He comes out faster for me than he would if I jabbed him with a pin.

"There is nothing Fury wouldn't do if I asked him to," his owner-trainer went on proudly. "Once he plunged into a ditch filled with water when his common sense would have told him to stay out. He does the acting and lets me worry about the danger."

Though Fury usually gets top billing, there are times when even a star must step into a minor role so that the show can go on. That was what happened when Fury responded to a call for help from Gene Nelson during the filming of the musical spectacular, *Oklahoma*. A scene in the script required Nelson to dance on top of a moving flat car. During the dance he was to whistle for his horse. The horse was supposed to slip the knot in the reins tied around a hitching rack, race over to the train tracks and gallop alongside the flat car so that Nelson, at the end of his dance, could swing into the saddle. Nelson did his part all right; it was the horse that spoiled the scene. They tried one horse after another with the same result. At last, in desperation, they sent for Fury. Fury and Mc-Cutcheon made a quick trip from Los Angeles to the picture location. The horse literally stepped out of his trailer and into the scene. He had no time to become familiar with his surroundings. The company was behind shooting schedule and every minute meant money lost.

McCutcheon explained to Fury what he was expected to do, then he rehearsed him once, just once. The cameras started to roll. Fury, on cue, slipped loose the tied reins, tore over to the moving train and kept a steady pace beside it while Gene Nelson leaped onto his back. One take and the scene was perfect. No human actor could do better than that.

McCutcheon admits that Fury is good. The big, black stallion earns more in a year than most human stars, but his owner wishes that he would be a little more modest. Fury is definitely a camera hog. On the set, he keeps edging forward to get close to the camera until he is practically hanging over the human actor's shoulder. One harassed director finally set up a dummy camera. Fury, unaware that there was no film in it, posed before it happily while the real camera shot the scenes with the rest of the cast.

"Horses," said Ralph McCutcheon, "are eager beavers. They want to work so badly you have to walk away in order to give them a rest. But I never stop in the middle of a lesson or when they've failed. I wait until they've completed their act and done it well. Always leave a horse on an up note. That's important."

It appears that horses need encouragement, just as we do.

Some trainers direct animals by motion, some

by voice. McCutcheon uses both gestures and verbal commands. Regardless of the method employed, it is a problem in communication. The majority of people seem to take it for granted that the animal should understand them, not they the animal. Rarely does one such as Henry Wynmalen stand forth to declare that since we are more intelligent—or think we are—the burden of understanding should be ours.

Yet how can we understand a horse or a dog? It cannot speak our language and we certainly cannot use the same means of communication it employs. Here we are in a position similar to that of the American tourist in Spain who stopped at a village inn for dinner. Desiring beefsteak but not knowing the Spanish word for it, he resorted to pantomime. Thrusting two fingers out from his forehead in imitation of a bull's horns, he pranced around the room snorting and pawing. The innkeeper watched him for a moment perplexed, then he brightened. *"Si, si, señor,"* he said, and hurried out. When he returned, he did not bring the beefsteak. He brought a ticket to the bullfights.

If humans who can give tongue to their thoughts are unable to understand each other, how much more difficult it is to set up communication with another specie. Trainers, such as Glen Randall, Jay Barry, Rudd Weatherwax, and Lee Duncan say that one must begin by studying the animal. Ralph McCutcheon has stated that he would not think of starting to train a horse until he had watched it at rest and at play. Only when he is thoroughly familiar with its natural disposition and abilities does he begin its schooling, for each horse is an individual, a personality, and no two can be trained in the same manner.

Horses, like dogs, live in a different world from ours, yet at many points they are astonishingly similar. Take the horse for example. It is a sociable animal. When left alone, it becomes morose and dull. It knows ambition in its desire to lead the herd. It knows reward when it becomes the leader, or is accepted into a particular herd. It knows punishment when it tries to push ahead where it does not socially belong or when it trespasses upon the territory of another horse. It knows fear and joy. It has a sense of humor, for horses are constantly playing tricks on each other. The mares are good, patient mothers, and it is a rare occurrence when one rejects or abandons her offspring. The stallions will fight to the death to protect the mares and their young. When cornered and unable to find safety in flight, the foals are bunched together and the stallions and mares form a protective ring around them, their backs to the enemy. In this position, they can let fly with their hind hoofs in a ripping, jolting back swing that will send a big boar bear sprawling.

Horses are as curious as we are, possibly more so. Humans especially arouse their curiosity, but they find it difficult to understand us. It bewilders them when we become irritated because they do

not immediately jump over the hurdles we have set up in the middle of a pasture for their training exercise. Why jump when it is so much easier to go around? They do not understand that we expect them to do tricks and race around a track for money. There is no money in their world. They are not impelled to save for a rainy day. Rain merely makes the grass grow that much greener.

To discover the differences between their world

and ours, we need only consider the horse's structure. Its legs are long and stiff, perfect for running but awkward for dancing. Its skin is thick and drawn tightly over the flesh. This makes it practically insensitive to all but intense pain. It can go crashing through brush that would tear a man to pieces and come out with only a few scratches. Due to its greater muscle power, it can outrun, outjump, and outwork us, and can withstand greater variations of heat and cold.

Man, laboring under the impression that the horse was created to carry him and work for him, would do well to remember that the horse is the oldest mammal upon earth. Its geneology goes back some forty million years. It roamed the world for millions of those years before man ever made his appearance upon the scene. It was a world of primeval freedom, of beauty and peace, of excitement and play, a world of lush meadows, wooded hills, cool running water. In it the wind talked to the horses and the horses ran with the wind. It was a world for which the horse was superbly designed, but it was never man's world, though he lived in the same surroundings. Man could pick up a stone and throw it, he could shape that stone into a weapon. This is impossible for the horse. It is not a matter of intelligence or lack of it. It is because the horse has hoofs instead of hands. It cannot pick up anything except with its teeth. Its knowledge of the world comes to it principally through its eyes, nose, and ears; it has no way of reaching out and feeling an object as we do. It cannot build a house, paint a picture, write a book, or play a musical instrument. It cannot even explore the shape of its own body. Since the horse is structurally unable to take part in human activities, it has no natural interest in the things of our world.

Many trainers constantly complain that it is difficult to catch and hold a horse's attention. Perhaps these trainers have failed to capture the horse's interest. Trigger, Champion, and Fury are eager to do what is required of them.

It is the same with dogs. Though closer to humans than horses, they too have a world of their own. They may come willingly into ours, but it is only by the door of affection. Rin Tin Tin and Lassie both adore their trainers. Lee Duncan is no more Rin's master than Rudd Weatherwax is Lassie's master. They are devoted friends.

In the last analysis, intelligence in animals may not be so much a question of mental ability as of communication, the establishing of mutual interests and mutual understanding.

8

More Than Courage

She was a beautiful German shepherd and her name was Kiss. Morris Frank, just twenty years old, six feet tall, and darkly handsome, could not visualize himself calling, "Here, Kiss! Come, Kiss!" He renamed her "Buddy." He knew that she was going to be his buddy as well as his eyes the moment he put his arms around her and felt a touch of her cold nose on his cheek. Right then he needed her assurance and affection as much as he needed her guidance.

He had come all the way from Nashville, Tennessee, to Fortunate Fields in Switzerland just for this dog, and the trip had been one long nightmare. Blindness made him dependent upon others, and as none of his family had been able to accompany him, he had been "shipped" by American Express as though he were a stamped and addressed package. The people who took him in charge handled him as unfeelingly as though he had been a package. He was not allowed to walk on deck except at certain times, and then only in the care of a steward. Every night at nine he was locked in his cabin and not released until breakfast the following morning. In Paris, where even a blind young man can find much that is pleasurable and exciting, Frank was thrust into a dingy hotel room and again the door was locked. Here he spent twenty-four miserable, lonely hours waiting for the train that would take him to Switzerland. It is no wonder that he arrived at his destination in a mood of bitterness and deep despair. Then he met Kiss who became his "Buddy," and Morris Frank's whole world changed.

Buddy was the first Seeing Eye dog to be trained at Fortunate Fields. Heretofore, the owner of this lovely Swiss estate, Dorothy Harrison Eustis, had concentrated on schooling dogs for police work, for army messenger and sentry duty, and the Red Cross. But she had seen trained dogs guide the blind in Potsdam, Germany, where a school for that purpose had been established, and she had written an article about it for the *Saturday Evening Post*.

Frank's father had read the article to his son, and the young man had immediately sent a letter to Mrs. Eustis asking if she could supply him with such a dog. In the letter he made a promise. He said that if he could obtain a Seeing Eye, he would devote his life to the founding of a school for guide dogs in America that the blind might be given "a chance for a new life." Mrs. Eustis could not resist that appeal. Buddy was her answer. When Frank arrived in Switzerland the dog was ready. There remained only the training of the man.

The schooling of both is arduous. The dog chosen to be a Seeing Eye, must pass an intelligence test "two or three points short of genius." It must have patience and willingness, and as with police and army dogs, a gaiety of disposition. Its first lessons are concerned with obedience. Then it must be taught to disobey. If its master orders, "Forward," and there is danger ahead, the dog must refuse to respond to the command. It must view the situation and make the decision that the blind man it is guiding cannot.

Gradually the dog learns to lead its instructor around all kinds of obstructions, including awnings thrust out over sidewalks. It is taught to weave its way through traffic, in to and out of elevators, up stairs and down. In the last month before graduation, the instructor puts a blindfold over his eyes and the dog is on its own. For four weeks the teacher walks in darkness, completely dependent upon the dog he has trained. Not until he is satisfied that his pupil is prepared to assume its great responsibility, does he turn the dog over to one who is really blind.

That exchange is not made, however, until the blind person is equally prepared to receive his

dog. Confidence comes slowly and it must be complete. The man must learn to obey the dog as much as the dog obeys the man, and when the dog has done something particularly praiseworthy, the man must not forget to give it lavish praise.

Morris Frank had been at Fortunate Fields only a few weeks when Buddy saved his life. The two were out walking in the nearby village of Vevey, discreetly followed by their instructor that he might explain, correct, and watch how both dog and man worked together. Suddenly they heard behind them the terrifying clamor of a runaway team of horses. They could not turn aside. The narrow street was hemmed in by high embankments. Had Buddy been impelled by instinct, she would have jerked free and outraced the horses to safety. Instead, she set her shoulders into the harness and went right up the seven-foot bank, hauling Frank with her. How to rescue a blind man from a runaway team had not been part of the dog's training. Somehow Buddy knew that the horses had gotten out of hand, and she instantly chose the one way of escape that would mean safety to the man she was guiding. This time Frank did not content himself with a pat and a hearty, "Good girl!" He got down on his knees and hugged her.

At last came the moment of parting from Mrs. Eustis and Fortunate Fields. Paris was the next stop. How would Buddy react to a place that was strange to her? Vevey had been her class room. She had known every foot of it before Frank arrived from America. But Paris is not a village, it is a great metropolis, bewildering even to human visitors.

Buddy took the capital of France in her stride. She led Frank into his hotel—this time a good one—and straight over to the clerk's desk. She indicated where the elevator button was located by pointing at it with her nose. Frank merely had to let his fingers follow the line of her poised head to land straight on target.

The dog soon learned to differentiate between the uniforms of bellboys, elevator operators, doormen, and police. No one told her, she worked it out for herself. Did Frank desire information, Buddy would lead him unerringly to the bell captain in the hotel or a policeman on the street. She did not know that in France they were called concierge and gendarme. She would not have cared. They were there and she blithely used them to aid her master.

Together man and dog visited Napoleon's tomb, sampled French food at a sidewalk café, and when the sun went down, made a tour of the night clubs. This time there was no locked door, no achingly lonely hours. Buddy and Frank were out on the town. Nor were there any locked cabins on the ship that took them back to the United States. Frank roamed the decks, made friends and danced with all the pretty girls on board. Buddy introduced him to them.

When they arrived in New York, Buddy had the distinction of being the first Seeing Eye dog in America. Newsmen who met her at the dock at first refused to believe that she could do all that Frank claimed. Under ordinary circumstances, the young man might have shrugged and gone his own way, but he had made a promise to Mrs. Eustis. If a Seeing Eye center was to be established in the United States, Buddy would have to make good—in print. Still it was largely Frank's pride and confidence in the dog that caused him to accept the reporters' challenge to be led by Buddy across any street in New York the men might name.

The reporters chose West street, a broad thoroughfare roaring with speeding cars, the equivalent of a freeway in the middle of Manhattan. If the thought occurred to these men that they might be sending Frank and Buddy to their deaths, it did not stop them. Here was the test they had decided upon for the Seeing Eye.

Buddy, just off the boat, with New York as foreign a city to her as Paris or London, calmly stepped into the thundering maelstrom of trucks and cars. She darted, side stepped, leaped between, around and in front of the racing juggernauts. Horns sounded, brakes squealed, alarmed drivers leaned out and cursed, but Buddy and Frank made it to the other side. As they reached the curb, a taxi drove up; out of it stepped a press photographer. He had been forced to take a cab in order to follow Buddy and her master. The rest of the reporters were still on the opposite side of the street. Not one had had sufficient courage to make his way through the stream of traffic that had been safely negotiated by a blind man and a dog. From then on, Buddy was so much in the news that Frank started a press scrapbook for her.

When Buddy became a Seeing Eye, she walked out of her own world and into the world of humans. She had to endure the taunts and insults of other dogs without fighting back. She could not chase cats or go darting off on exciting scent trails except when her master removed her harness. Even then, she never let Frank out of her sight. She was on duty twenty-four hours a day, every day in the year.

Animal psychologists say that the devotion of a dog to its master is instinctive. The Lupu, or wolf breed of dog such as the German shepherd, simply transfers to man the loyalty that its ancestor felt for the leader of the pack. The need of the dog for close companionship with humans is explained as an instinctive effort to compensate for the loss of the social life of the pack and the sense of security the ancestral wolf found in running with it.

These statements are somewhat bewildering in view of the fact that men who have spent their lives in the wilderness as guides and hunters insist that wolves do not run in packs. Occasionally one may glimpse four or five wolves together, but this does not constitute a pack in the sense of a general gathering of these animals. The members of a group of wolves all belong to the same family. There is the father, mother, a couple of half-grown youngsters, and the new cubs. Even these do not come together unless there is a scarcity of food, for as a rule the wolf is a solitary hunter.

To continue the disillusionment, these men, whites and Indians alike, insist that wolves, especially the big timber wolves, are exceedingly shy. Let one catch a whiff of man's scent and it fades like a ghost into the forest.

As for the stories of wolves stalking humans, naturalists such as William J. Long, have checked every contemporary account of wolf attacks upon people both in America and Europe, and have not found one based upon provable evidence. Russian wolves, they say, may be different. They have been unable to obtain any information on this subject from behind the Iron Curtain.

These woodsmen also maintain that while in a family group one wolf always leads, the leader is not the ferocious male to be found in fiction. It is the female. Mamma, not papa, gives the orders, and for a very good reason. The female is more wary and cunning than the male. She has had to be. Upon her is the burden of feeding and protecting the young.

If what these naturalists claim is true, then how can a dog inherit a sense of loyalty for the leader of the pack when wolves do not normally run in packs? Nor does the picture of the wolf as a solitary hunter offer any clue as to the dog's need of human companionship.

It may be that our image of wolves has been created out of myths and legends. If ancient man at first did not fear these animals, as archeologists believe, that fear may have arisen when mankind settled in communities and began to pen their flocks and herds. Then indeed the farmer would have had good reason to dread the wolf that came down on the fold. Undoubtedly that dread was given shape and made huge in fireside stories on those wintry nights when wild game was scarce and the wolf slipped out of the forest to seek the food that could not run from it because of corral bars.

In any event, it seems necessary to find new reasons for the dog's loyalty and desires, but then the theory of the pack never did answer all the questions. For instance, why does the dog so greatly need affection and praise? We can be sure that its wolf ancestors, in or out of packs, did not go around patting each other on the head and barking approval of deeds well done, yet all canine trainers say that a dog values praise and petting far more than a reward of food.

Perhaps this great need of the dog came into being when long ago man took it from its natural world and brought it into his own. Here the dog is a stranger. It is as much a stranger as the horse and for the same reason. The physical structure of the dog prevents it from either understanding or taking an active part in human affairs save at those points where the dog is used for hunting, herding, trailing and guarding. Feeling itself in an alien world, the dog would naturally require constant assurance and companionship, as we would were we slaves to a higher intelligence whose motives and actions we could not comprehend.

Like any other dog, Buddy demanded her dole of appreciation, but she did not need anyone to assure her that she had done well. She was fully aware of it without being told. After successfully completing some exceptionally difficult act, she would prance around happily, wriggling in undisguised approval of her own cleverness. However, she did not consider herself particularly clever when, for the second time, she saved her master's life.

Frank, coming out of his hotel room in a hurry to meet a business engagement, made straight for

the elevator. The doors opened and he gave the command, "Forward." Buddy did not stir. Frank repeated the order. Again Buddy ignored it. Then Frank made the mistake of dropping the harness lead and starting forward alone, thinking to force the dog to follow. Instantly Buddy flung herself against his legs, pressing him back. At that moment a woman screamed. It was a hotel maid coming along the hall. "Don't move, Mr. Frank!" she cried. "The elevator isn't there." Another step and Morris Frank would have plunged to his death down the elevator shaft.

Though Frank heaped exaggerated praise upon the dog, Buddy considered her action simply as part of the day's work. She could see no difference between a hole in a building and one in the street, around which she had often led her master. She had been taught to do that. It was really not a test of her cleverness and ingenuity.

Though many of Buddy's acts can be explained as the result of instinct plus training, an equal number appear to be both highly intelligent and intuitive. One of her amazing abilities was the instant recognition of the intent of a person. She went straight for a thief who was trying to break into the Frank house, yet when Frank himself was held up one night in a dark alley, Buddy never moved a muscle. Her master was both thankful and puzzled. Had Buddy jumped the man, she undoubtedly would have been shot, but Frank could not understand why the dog had not sprung to his defense—until the thief was caught and identified as an inmate of an insane asylum. Apparently Buddy was aware of the difference between a person who knew what he was doing and one who was not mentally responsible.

Neither instinct nor any amount of training prepares a dog to read the minds of her master's girl friends, yet that is what Buddy did. If a girl wanted to go to a dance or motion picture, Buddy would cross to the door and stand there until Frank was forced to get his hat. Should the girl wish for a quiet evening at home listening to music, Buddy would climb onto the couch and lie down. The girls did not verbally express their desires; they did not have to. Buddy knew what they preferred and aided Frank's romances by indicating what he should do to win the approval of the young ladies. Moreover, Buddy never made a single mistake in her mind-reading act.

She seemed equally aware that the success of a Seeing Eye center in America depended upon the way she conducted herself. On Frank's lecture tours, Buddy knew that she was the star attraction, and she appeared on the platform beside him with all the poise and charm of a star. She stressed important points in Frank's speech by woofing, and sometimes she woofed to attract the wandering attention of the audience.

At private interviews when Frank appealed to wealthy individuals for donations to the cause, Buddy would establish herself where she could look directly at the man, and she kept on looking at him while Frank talked. It was her proud, direct, insistent gaze, as much as Frank's powers of persuasion that caused high level executives to reach for their check books.

The perfection of her conduct in public so impressed restaurant owners that they agreed to permit Seeing Eyes into their establishments, regardless of the sign, "No Dogs Allowed." Railroad officials only had to meet Buddy and watch her work to announce that the iron-bound rule of all carriers forbidding dogs to ride except as baggage need not apply to the Seeing Eye. Buddy convinced them that some dogs had better manners than most humans.

Her last official act was to win the consent of United Airlines to Seeing Eye dogs traveling in planes as paid passengers. She was then so old and ill that she could scarcely stand, but she went through her performance flawlessly. It was as though she realized that where she led all the guide dogs in the world would follow.

Buddy offered all her loyalty and devotion to the blind man who had been given into her care. Responsibility for his life and happiness was not a burden upon her, it was an act of love. This, as much as the work she did to aid the cause, more than earned her the title Morris Frank bestowed upon her—"The First Lady of the Seeing Eye."

9

The Answer

In the opinion of the experts, do the lives of these heroic dogs and champion horses prove that they acted upon instinct plus training, or were they motivated by intelligent reasoning?

The question as yet cannot be fully answered. First must come certain other questions, such as: What is instinct? What is intelligence? Where does one end and the other begin? To what ex-

tent do people *respond to instinct plus training rather than intelligent reasoning?*

Trainers of dogs and horses say that one must have the same patience with these animals as with a six-year-old child, but does this indicate a lack of intelligence, or that the dog and horse cannot speak our language and we cannot converse in theirs?

It is sobering to think, as Barbara Woodhouse suggests, that animals may have been trying to communicate with us since the day they left their primeval freedom and came into our world. If so, they may be as appalled by our seeming stupidity as we are frustrated by theirs.

The most important tool humanity possesses is language. With it, man conquered the earth. Unfortunately, for the first hundred thousand years he was so busy shaping and polishing that tool he did not stop to ask if all the other forms of life about him might not have a language, too. It is only recently that men have had sufficient leisure to investigate this field, yet even in this short space of time they can say with certainty, "Yes, each has some means of communication, but we do not always understand the method used. However, we know that the horse and the dog are more intuitive than we are. They understand what we feel far better than what we say."

All authorities agree that these animals respond with amazing eagerness to those who approach them with sympathy and kindness. In the

words of Eliza Doolittle in George Bernard Shaw's Pygmalion: *"The difference between a lady and a flower girl is not how she behaves, but how she's treated."* The difference between a dumb animal and an intelligent one may lie in the approach.

Treat a horse or a dog as though it were capable of intelligent reasoning and that encouragement may mark the beginning of a new means of communication, not between animal and man but between friend and friend, who are separated only by the barrier of language, of understanding.

"No truth appears to me more evident," declared David Hume in his Treatise on Human Nature, *"than that the beasts are endowed with thought and reason as well as men. The arguments are in this case so obvious that they never escape the most stupid and ignorant."*

Do horses possess intelligence?

Do dogs possess intelligence?

What do you *think?*

Famous
Classics

Alice in Wonderland

Fifty Famous Fairy Stories

Little Men

Robinson Crusoe

Five Little Peppers and How They Grew

Treasure Island

The Wonderful Wizard of Oz

The Three Musketeers

Robin Hood

Heidi

Little Women

Black Beauty

Huckleberry Finn

Tom Sawyer

Meet wonderful friends—in the books
that are favorites—year after year

Fiction for Young People

THE RIFLEMAN

THE RESTLESS GUN

WAGON TRAIN

GENE AUTRY
The Ghost Riders

WYATT EARP

GUNSMOKE

ROY ROGERS
The Enchanted Canyon

DALE EVANS
Danger in Crooked Canyon

ROY ROGERS AND DALE EVANS
River of Peril

DRAGNET

BOBBSEY TWINS
Merry Days Indoors and Out
At the Seashore
In the Country

WALTON BOYS
Gold in the Snow
Rapids Ahead

ANNIE OAKLEY
Danger at Diablo
Double Trouble

NOAH CARR, YANKEE FIREBRAND

LEE BAIRD, SON OF DANGER

CIRCUS BOY
Under the Big Top
War on Wheels

HAVE GUN, WILL TRAVEL

MAVERICK

ASSIGNMENT IN SPACE
WITH RIP FOSTER

DONNA PARKER
At Cherrydale
Special Agent
On Her Own

TROY NESBIT'S
MYSTERY ADVENTURES
The Diamond Cave Mystery
Mystery at Rustlers' Fort

RED RYDER
Adventures at Chimney Rock

RIN TIN TIN
Rinty
Call to Danger
The Ghost Wagon Train

FURY
The Mystery at Trappers' Hole

LASSIE
Mystery at Blackberry Bog
The Secret of the Summer
Forbidden Valley

WALT DISNEY
Spin and Marty
Spin and Marty, Trouble at Triple-R

TRIXIE BELDEN
The Gatehouse Mystery
The Red Trailer Mystery
The Mystery off Glen Road
The Mysterious Visitor
Mystery in Arizona

Adventure! Mystery! Read these exciting
stories written especially for young readers